What God Requires

Learning to Do Life His Way

A Bible Study Workbook
by Matthew Allen

Published by
Spiritbuilding Publishers
9700 Ferry Road, Waynesville, Ohio 45068

WHAT GOD REQUIRES I
Learning to Do Life His Way
By Matthew Allen

All Scripture references are taken from Holman Bible Publishers'
Christian Standard Bible unless otherwise noted.

ISBN: 978–1–964–80522–1

Spiritbuilding
PUBLISHERS

spiritbuilding.com

Table of Contents

Stressing the Need for Obedience

I n the 90s, the FAA tested the strength of airplane windshields by using a gun that launched a dead chicken straight at the plane's windshield at the approximate speed at which the plane flew. If the windshield didn't crack from the impact of the flying chicken, then it was thought that it would survive an actual collision with a bird in flight. Soon, British officials found out about this testing and wanted to conduct something similar with a locomotive they were developing. They borrowed the FAA's chicken gun, loaded the chicken, and fired. The ballistic chicken shattered the windshield, went through the engineer's chair, and smashed the instrument panel behind, embedding itself into the back wall of the engine cab. The British were stunned. They asked the FAA to conduct their test again and see if everything was done correctly. The FAA reviewed the test thoroughly and had only one recommendation … "Thaw the chicken."

There is a right way to do things. If we do things the wrong way, no matter the intention, chaos results. The same principle applies to the church and Christian life. We must obey God, submitting to what He says and how He says to do it. What He tells us to do is revealed in Scripture.

This is the foundation of Christian living. Not only does the great commission charge us with preaching and making disciples as we go, Matthew 28:19, it also instructs us to teach others all that Jesus has commanded, 28:20. People must not only believe but obey or submit to God's commands.

- John 8:31: "If you continue in my word, you really are my disciples."
- John 14:15: "If you love me, you will keep my commands."
- 1 John 2:3–6: "This is how we know that we know him: if we keep his commands. The one who says, "I have come to know him," and

yet doesn't keep his commands, is a liar, and the truth is not in him. But whoever keeps his word, truly in him the love of God is made complete. This is how we know we are in him: The one who says he remains in him should walk just as he walked."

If a person claims he loves, believes, and belongs to God, then it will be reflected in the way he obeys God. When we came to Christ for salvation, we made a commitment to obey without equivocating, resisting, or compromising. This, of course, is obedience from the heart.

Not Legalism

When stressing the need for obedience, we must never allow our emphasis to drift into legalism. The term *legalism* has its origin in the work of Edwin Fisher (d. 1655) known as *The Marrow of Modern Divinity*. In it, Fisher used the term to describe "one who bringeth the Law into the case of Justification." While the term is never found in either Testament, the idea certainly is.[1] A simple way to describe *legalism* is preoccupation with form at the expense of substance. It works on the outside and drives people to conform *externally*. It holds that salvation depends on total obedience to the letter of the law and often displays excessive concern for minute details … while neglecting the spirit of the law.

Legalism also refers to those who add a list of dos and don'ts to biblical commands. Usually, this is done to help prevent a person from violating biblical commands. But soon, these lists take on equal authority with God's commandments … and even, in some cases, supersede them. The effects of legalism often lead to grave fear that forces people to conform externally or be lost.

---

1   Deasley, A. R. G. "Legalism." Pages 478–9 in *Evangelical Dictionary of Biblical Theology*. Electronic ed. Baker Reference Library. Grand Rapids: Baker Book House, 1996.

From the Heart

In Romans 6:17, Paul commends the Roman Christians for the way they came to Christ. He says: *But thank God that, although you used to be slaves of sin, you obeyed from the heart that pattern of teaching to which you were handed over.*

Note how the Romans were motivated out of the heart to obediently respond to the gospel. *From the heart* describes a very personal decision one makes by his own volition to surrender to God. But Paul's words go further. He is not speaking of superficial or coerced obedience, but rather something deeply felt and deeply motivated from deep inside someone.[2] The Christian reality is a matter of the heart. Paul focused on this in at least two other places in Romans:

- Romans 5:5: This hope will not disappoint us, because God's love has been poured out in our hearts through the Holy Spirit who was given to us.
- Romans 10:9–10: If you confess with your mouth, "Jesus is Lord," and believe in your heart that God raised him from the dead, you will be saved. One believes with the heart, resulting in righteousness, and one confesses with the mouth, resulting in salvation.

The issue is not being conformed to what is expected on the outside; the issue is the condition of our heart … i.e., doing *God's will from your heart,* Ephesians 6:6. Obedience is a commitment to change from the inside out. It is a long-term commitment, not a short-term fix. It is the lifelong work of forming the kind of convictions, motives, and attitudes that move a person to do the work of God from the heart.

It is seen in the way one respects the word of God:

---

2   Dunn, James D. G. *Romans 1–8.* Vol. 38A. Word Biblical Commentary. Dallas: Word, Incorporated, 1988, p. 343.

For the word of God is living and effective and sharper than any double-edged sword, penetrating as far as the separation of soul and spirit, joints and marrow. It is able to judge the thoughts and intentions of the heart, Hebrews 4:12.

The Word penetrates the heart … all the way to our thoughts and intentions. The Word produces conviction. It reveals the source of our thoughts and intentions, unmasking their actual condition. It cuts open and reveals the true state. It has the power to cut away what is bad, cleanse our hearts, and help us draw near to God with a heartfelt response.

…let us draw near with a true heart in full assurance of faith, with our hearts sprinkled clean from an evil conscience and our bodies washed in pure water, Hebrews 10:22.

Obedience Is the Fruit of Your Relationship with God

Your salvation was an act of obedience. *You have purified yourselves by your obedience to the truth,* 1 Peter 1:22. You were born again by responding to the truth of the gospel communicated through the Word of God, 1 Peter 1:23. That truth is communicated in Acts 2:38. Repentance and baptism are commands that must be obeyed. When you complied in faith, God saved you because you reached out in utter necessity. There was no way you could save yourself.

Your salvation was not only an act of obedience at the beginning, on the occasion of your baptism, but it was a pledge of continued obedience, recognizing that Jesus is Lord over your life. You made the commitment to follow in obedience. It is the purpose of your salvation. Peter speaks of his relationship with God as he mentions his being part of the people chosen by the foreknowledge of God through the sanctifying work of the Spirit, for the purpose of obedience, sprinkled with the blood of Christ, 1 Peter 1:2. Why was Peter saved? Answer: *To be obedient.*

Paul also made this point in Ephesians. You were saved by grace through faith, 2:8, and not by your own work, 2:9. Your re-creation, by God, was for the purpose of *good works, which God prepared ahead of time for us to do,* 2:10. From before time, God not only chose a people to be in relationship with Himself, but He marked out a path for them to walk. This is a path of good works, which characterize their lives and bring glory to Him. Your works are an outgrowth of your salvation. It is your faith that produces the works, and it is out of love that you labor, 1 Thessalonians 1:3. Your obedience doesn't negate God's grace … it confirms it. It is evidence of God's saving work going on inside your heart. By His grace and the power of His word, He has given you a heart that wants to obey.

It is true that one will not be saved without an obedient response from the heart. *Faith without works is dead,* James 2:26. A lack of an obedient or compliant heart is evidence of someone who has not committed to God. But as we obey, let us never take credit for salvation. The spirit of *I am doing these things to be saved* is nothing more than legalism. Your works do nothing to improve your status or position *in Christ.* Again, we refer to Ephesians 2:8–10.

- You have already been saved, 2:8.
- You did not and will not save yourself, 2:9.
- The works you do in Christ are evidence of having been re-created, 2:10.

All your work in Christ is the fruit of the Spirit, who dwells within you, Galatians 5:22–23. He gets all the glory in your obedience. You are simply a servant obeying the wishes of your Lord.

In This Study

What are some of the things God has called us to do? What are things that we must observe by way of growth and maturity? While not intended to be exhaustive, the lessons provided cover principles from both Testaments and go far in helping us understand how to please our God as He rules over our lives.

May we come to a better understanding of the need to respect God and His word, seeing the importance of doing life His way. Life works out better when we pay attention to how God wishes for us to comply. Do you have a heart that is ready to obey?

Lesson 1

Love the Lord with All Your Heart

He said to him, "Love the Lord your God with all your heart, with all your soul, and with all your mind. This is the greatest and most important command, Matthew 22:37–38.

Introduction

Beginning in Matthew 22:34–36, Jesus is approached by a Pharisee[3], *an expert in the law,* who tests Him by asking which is the greatest commandment. This is after Jesus had silenced the Sadducees. Now, they conspire together on another way to defeat Him. It is the perfect fulfillment of Psalm 2:2:

> The kings of the earth take their stand, and the rulers conspire together against the Lord and his Anointed One:

The lawyer's question, *which command in the law is the greatest,* was a common practice by the Jews who made many efforts to summarize the law.

- David summarized the law in 11 commands in Psalm 15.
- Isaiah specified 6 in Isaiah 33:15.
- Micah recited 3 in Micah 6:8.
- Isaiah cites 2 in Isaiah 56:1
- Habakkuk reduced them all to one in Habakkuk 2:4.[4]

---

3   Mark 12.28 describes this expert in the law as a Scribe.

4   *The New Daily Study Bible: The Gospel of Mark.* The New Daily Study Bible. Edinburgh: Saint Andrew Press, 2001, p. 342.

Around twenty years before Christ, Rabbi Hillel was approached by a Gentile convert to Judaism who asked him to summarize the whole law while he stood on one leg (an expression which means to summarize quickly). Hillel's answer was a negative version of the *Golden Rule*, "What you hate for yourself, do not to your neighbor. This is the whole law; all the rest is commentary. Go and learn it."[5] Both before and after Jesus, rabbis answered this question in different ways. One said Proverbs 3:6 is the heart of the law: *in all your ways acknowledge him, and he will make straight your paths.*

Now, back to our story. Considering Mark's account, this is not a generic question with innocent motives. The lawyer is looking for a way to charge Jesus with blasphemy. The scribes said Moses received 613 commands in the law, with 248 being affirmative and 365 being negative.[6] The lawyer wanted to know which of these should have been ranked first. Which of the other commands weren't as important? Jesus provides His answer without hesitation. Some say this is the most straightforward response of all of Jesus' answers to questions He was asked.

The command Jesus quotes in 22:37 was part of the Shema, which was made up of Deuteronomy 6:4–9, 11:13–21, and Numbers 15:37–41. Every devoted Jew in Jesus' day would have recited the Shema twice each day. Orthodox Jews wrote these passages out and placed them in small boxes (the *mezuzah*) fastened to their doorposts so they would be reminded of it as they went in and out of their house. See Deuteronomy 6:9; 11:20. They also placed them in their phylacteries, small leather boxes they fastened to their foreheads, to always keep the word on their mind. The basis for wearing phylacteries comes from Deuteronomy 6:8. Mezuzahs and phylacteries are both still used by devout Jews today.

---

5   Barclay, p. 341.

6   Augsburger, Myron S., and Lloyd J. Ogilvie. *Matthew*. Vol. 24 of *The Preacher's Commentary Series*. Nashville, TN: Thomas Nelson Inc, 1982, p. 18.

Jesus' Answer:
The Combining of Two Commands

The first command Jesus quotes in Matthew 22:37 is Deuteronomy 6:5, one that everyone would have agreed upon. Love God. *This is the greatest and most important command,* 22:38. He then, in 22:39, quotes Leviticus 19:18. Love your neighbor. Then He adds:

> All the Law and the Prophets depend on these two commands, Matthew 22:40.

This verse is especially important as He includes both the Law *and* the Prophets, which was larger than what the Sadducees recognized.[7] On these two commands hang everything else in the Law and Prophets. God's desire is for us to love Him *and* others. The only way to prove our love for God is by showing love for others.[8]

Love God

The word for *love* in Deuteronomy 6:5 (the passage Jesus quotes from) refers mainly to an act of the will and mind. While emotion may certainly be involved, the most important characteristics of this love are someone's dedication and commitment of choice. *It is a love of action.* It is a love of purpose and self-sacrifice. It is a whole-being response.

Heart, soul, and mind

In Hebrew, *heart* involves the core of one's identity. From the heart spring our thoughts, words, and actions. *Keep your heart with all vigilance, for from it flow the springs of life,* Proverbs 4:23.

---

7   The Sadducees only recognized the Torah as authoritative.

8   Barclay, William. *The Gospel of Matthew.* Third Ed. The New Daily Study Bible. Edinburgh: Saint Andrew Press, 2001, p. 345.

We are to love God with all our *soul*. This word can refer to our emotions, see Matthew 26:38. There is an emotional component in our relationship with God, and it should be fully employed in our devotion to Him.

We must love God with all our *mind*. This word has to do with our purposes and intentions. We must move our will to get on board with God's plan.

We should also include Mark's addition as he includes the word *strength*, Mark 12:30. God is calling for the highest form of sacrifice—our entire self, with all our physical capabilities.

From this we learn:

- Our love for God is *intelligent.*
- It has *feeling.*
- It is *willing.*
- It is *serving.*[9]

Listed Distinctly

Note how loving God with our heart, soul, and mind are not joined together. *They are spread apart.* We are to love God *with all* our heart, *with all* our soul, and *with all* our mind. This is meant to express the greatest amount possible. God is not looking for someone who simply wants to go through the motions or perform a few rituals to check off a list. God's wholehearted love "must not be answered in a halfhearted manner."[10] His sons and daughters are to be characterized by *whole-being* love for Him. We are to love God with everything we are.

---

9   MacArthur, John F., Jr. *Matthew*. MacArthur New Testament Commentary. Chicago: Moody Press, 1985, Vol. 3, p. 339.

10   Hendriksen, *Exposition of the Gospel According to Matthew*, p. 809

Love and Obedience Go Together

God shows His faithfulness by keeping *his gracious covenant loyalty for a thousand generations with those who love him and keep his commands*, Deuteronomy 7:9. Jesus said: "If you love me, you will keep my commandments," John 14:15. Paul spoke of our need to have an *undying love* in Ephesians 6:24. An unbeliever is *anyone* who *does not love the Lord*, 1 Corinthians 16:22.

Even though we fall short by failing to always do right, our hearts should always love what is right and long to do what honors God. The one who loves God with all his heart, soul, and mind is someone who trusts and obeys. This is seen by:

- Meditating on God's glory, Psalm 18:1–3.
- Trusting in God's divine power, Psalm 31:23.
- Seeking fellowship with God, Psalm 63:1–8.
- Loving God's law, Psalm 119:165.
- Being sensitive to how God feels, Psalm 69:9.
- Loving what God loves, Psalm 119:72, 97, 103.
- Loving whom God loves, 1 John 5:1.
- Hating what God hates, Psalm 97:10.
- Grieving over sin, Matthew 26:75.
- Rejecting the world, 1 John 2:15.
- Longing to be with Christ, 2 Timothy 4:8.
- Obeying God wholeheartedly, John 14:21.[11]

Love is the true secret of effective obedience to God. A loving heart will not find His commandments to be burdensome, 1 John 5:3. Love will chase away the fear of punishment, 1 John 4:18. Love will take pleasure in following His commands, Romans 7:22; Psalm 119:70 and find sadness when transgressing them, Matthew 5:4. Those who love God from the heart obey in the most effective way.

---

11   MacArthur, *Ibid.*, p. 340.

An Impossible Command?

The absolute love Jesus calls for is beyond our human ability. We love God, not in perfection or completeness, but totally … with heart, soul, and mind. We will always be reaching forward toward the goal of a more perfect love … growing and maturing … but until we shed our human body with its frailties and weaknesses, this love will never be all it should be. As we go forward in our spiritual life, let us commit to walk by the Spirit, Galatians 5:16. We also should determine to cooperate fully with the Spirit as He performs the work of transformation in our heart, Galatians 5:22–23. We must never grieve Him (Ephesians 4:30) or stifle His work (1 Thessalonians 5:19).

We grow in love by cooperating with the Spirit. We cooperate by practicing the spiritual disciplines of reading the Word, giving, and serving. What are some things you can do this week to improve your practice of these things?

The sum of the revealed Word of God is the command to love God and to love Him before all others, more than anything and anyone else.[12]

---

12   O'Donnell, Douglas Sean. *Matthew: All Authority in Heaven and on Earth.* Edited by R. Kent Hughes. Preaching the Word. Wheaton, IL: Crossway, 2013, p. 658.

For Thought and Reflection

1. Why did the lawyer ask Jesus the question in 22:36?

2. What does Jesus mean by "love"? See also John 14:15; 15:13; Philippians 2:3–4.

3. Since the love Jesus describes is beyond our ability, what hope do we have to love like this? What can we learn from Paul's teaching in Galatians 5:14–16; 22–23?

4. Think about last week. In what ways did you fall short of the command to love God with all your heart, soul, and mind?

5. What good habit will you invest time in this week so that God's spirit can grow your love?

Lesson 2

Love Your Neighbor as Yourself

The second is like it: Love your neighbor as yourself. All the
Law and the Prophets depend on these two commands,"
Matthew 22:39–40.

Introduction

Previously, we examined the first great commandment, Matthew
22:37: *Love the Lord your God with all your heart, with all your
soul, and with all your mind.* Then Jesus does something not
done before. With authority, He inseparably ties Leviticus 19:18 to his
answer.[13] By doing so, He answers how one proves his love for God. True
love for God demonstrates itself in sacrificial love and service to others.
Neither command is to be raised above the other. The second great
command is equal to the first. In fact, it is linked to it. The force of each
depends on the other.

Love Others

The love in 22:39 is the same kind of love mentioned in v. 37. Genuine
love for others reveals itself by the choices it makes. Sentiment or
emotion may play a role, but more so, it is a love driven by purpose,
intention, and action.

---

13   There are some Jewish texts where we see these two ideas tied together. These
extrabiblical writings are thought to have come after Jesus, but some date them before
Christ. Three examples are found in the *Testaments of the Twelve Patriarchs.* The
Testament of Dan, 5:3 says: *Throughout all your life love the Lord, and one another with a
true heart.* See Charlesworth, James H. *The Old Testament Pseudepigrapha.* Vol. 1. New
York; London: Yale University Press, 1983, Vol. 1, p. 809.

Let's refer to the Leviticus command:

> Do not take revenge or bear a grudge against members of your community, but love your neighbor as yourself; I am the Lord, Leviticus 19:18.

Looking back at Leviticus 19:16-17, love is the answer for the refusal to slander someone else. Love is the solution for the bad behavior of taking revenge or holding a grudge. Love is the counter to harboring anger or resentment in your heart. It is a conscious choice that does not always involve warm sentiments or emotions. Also, in Leviticus 19, we find instructions on not stealing, dealing falsely, lying, swearing falsely by God's name, defrauding others, placing a stumbling block before the blind, or rendering unjust judgment. Loving our neighbor as ourselves is the antidote to these things.

How this love is measured

Note that the amount of love we pour out to others is to be in the same amount as we love our self. In other words, just as you already love yourself, care for yourself, and think about yourself, you are to love your neighbor in the same way.[14] When we are hungry, we see that we are fed. When we are thirsty, we find something to drink. If we are suffering, we look for a remedy … because the priority is self-care. A person never dismisses his own needs, *for no one ever hates his own flesh but provides and cares for it,* Ephesians 5:29. We value our own personal welfare. It is part of the human condition. As you love yourself, love others.

We must not separate love for God from loving our neighbor. It is incredibly easy to do. We can worship God in church on Sunday, praising Him, and yet act rudely and condemn someone who doesn't drive like we do on the way home. We deceive ourselves into thinking that how we treat others has no bearing on our relationship with God. Yet, how

---

14   Courson, Jon. *Jon Courson's Application Commentary.* Nashville, TN: Thomas Nelson, 2003, p. 164.

we treat others is how we treat God. The supreme obligation to God includes a duty to love and care for our fellow man.

Barclay has written:

> It is only when we love God that other people become lovable. The biblical teaching about human beings is not that we are collections of chemical elements, not that we are part of the brute creation, but that men and women are made in the image of God (Genesis 1:26–27). It is for that reason that human beings are lovable. The true basis of all democracy is in fact the love of God. Take away the love of God, and we can look at human nature and become angry at those who cannot be taught; we can become pessimistic about those who cannot make progress; we can become callous to those who are cold and calculating in their actions. The love of humanity is firmly grounded in the love of God.

> To be truly religious is to love God and to love those whom God made in his own image; and to love God and other people, not with a vague sentimentality, but with that total commitment which issues in devotion to God and practical service of others.[15]

On These Two, Every Other Law Hangs

Everything else God requires is summed up in these two dual commands. Imagine two pegs upon which garments hang; these great laws uphold all the other precepts in the Law and the Prophets. Every command of God will fall under one or the other of these, and all the subsequent instructions show us how to fulfill them. The New Testament declares:

> Dear friends, let us love one another, because love is from God, and everyone who loves has been born of God and knows

15   Barclay, William. *The Gospel of Matthew*. Third Ed. The New Daily Study Bible. Edinburgh: Saint Andrew Press, 2001, p. 324–5.

God. The one who does not love does not know God, because God is love, 1 John 4:7–8.

Do not owe anyone anything, except to love one another, for the one who loves another has fulfilled the law. The commandments, Do not commit adultery; do not murder; do not steal; do not covet; and any other commandment, are summed up by this commandment: Love your neighbor as yourself. Love does no wrong to a neighbor. Love, therefore, is the fulfillment of the law, Romans 13:8–10.

MacArthur writes:

If people loved perfectly there would be no need for law, because the person who loves others will never do them harm. In the same way, the believer who loves God with all his being will never take His name in vain, will never worship idols, and will never fail to obey, worship, honor, and glorify Him as Lord.[16]

What This Looks Like

Loving your neighbor is not always easy. We often must choose to follow through. We need to be intentional. What are some ways we can demonstrate love to our neighbor?

- **Move with compassion**. We cannot sit by when someone else suffers a need. Will we help according to our ability?
- **Look out for the well-being of others**. We need to pay attention. We need to think of their needs.
- **Seize opportunities to serve**. Love is kindness in action.
- **Speak kindly**. Words build up or tear down, so use words to build others up. Encourage them.

---

16   MacArthur, Matthew, Vol. 3, p. 342.

- **Magnify the good**. Pay compliments. Speak your appreciation.
- **Give others the benefit of the doubt**. Don't take offense easily. *Imperfect people often do dumb things, including yourself.*
- **Share in the joys and sorrows of others**. Be there with your heart open with arms wide in support.
- **Practice forgiveness**. Forgive others as you have been forgiven.

For Thought and Reflection

1. How can we demonstrate genuine love for God?

2. Why do you think Jesus commanded us to love our neighbor? Is it always easy to love our neighbor? Explain.

3. How could you tie Matthew 7:12 together with the second-greatest commandment? Do they fit? Explain.

4. Barclay said: "It is only when we love God that other people become lovable." What does this statement mean to you?

5. Look back over the seven bullet points of the previous section. Find a Scripture or two that supports each point.

Self-Examination

Test yourselves to see if you are in the faith. Examine yourselves. Or do you yourselves not recognize that Jesus Christ is in you?—unless you fail the test, 2 Corinthians 13:5.

Introduction

One of the more famous sayings of Socrates (d. 399 B.C.) is "The unexamined life is not worth living for human beings." He made this statement after having been condemned to death for going against the ruling elite of Athens who charged him with corrupting the minds of his youthful students. He had discovered that one of life's most important tasks is not to examine others … but to examine oneself. While Socrates spoke purely from the perspective of human wisdom and philosophy, the idea of the examined life is very much a biblical principle.

Self-examination is the study and examination of one's behavior, qualities, conduct, and motivations; introspection. Regular and intentional self-examination is an important aspect of the healthy Christian life. Through self-examination, the Spirit enables us to honestly review our motives, thinking patterns, beliefs, behaviors, etc., to see whether they align with the Word of God. Self-examination isn't about making us feel good about ourselves or tearing ourselves down entirely. It's about identifying our faults so that we can change and become more like God.

The Biblical Basis for Self-Examination

David is a great example

In numerous instances, the Psalmist prayed for the Lord to examine his heart:

- In the opening verses of Psalm 17, David asked the Lord to vindicate his heart by testing and examining it. He says that God had tried him and found nothing evil. David was committed to keeping his steps on the pathway of God, Psalm 17:1-6.
- In Psalm 26:2, he asks God to *test me ... and try me; examine my heart and mind.*
- In Psalm 77:6, David speaks about his personal reflection and heart examination: *I meditate in my heart, and my spirit ponders.*
- David also asked God to *search me, ... and know my heart. Test me and know my concerns. See if there is any offensive way in me; lead me into the everlasting way,* Psalm 139:23–24.

Other passages

- As the destruction of Judah was coming down in full force, Jerusalem was destroyed; Jeremiah urged the people to look inward: *Let's examine and probe our ways, and turn back to the Lord,* Lamentations 3:40.
- Haggai urged the people of his land to *think carefully about your ways,* Haggai 1:7. This prophet repeatedly stresses the need for the people to *think carefully,* using those words at least three times in his short book, 1:7; 2:15, 18.
- Before partaking of the Lord's supper, Paul said *let a person examine himself, ... for whoever eats and drinks without recognizing the body, eats and drinks judgment on himself,* 1 Corinthians 11:28a, 29.

- 2 Corinthians 13:5: *Test yourselves ...*
- Hebrews 3:12: *Watch out, brothers and sisters, so that there won't be in any of you an evil, unbelieving heart that turns away from the living God.*

Self-Examination is not Easy

Are We Blind to Our Own Shortcomings?

All a person's ways seem right to him, but the Lord weighs hearts, Proverbs 21:2. Jeremiah said in 17:9: *The heart is more deceitful than anything else, and incurable—who can understand it?*

The fallen human condition glories in itself. We thrive on self-centeredness, self-righteousness, self-sufficiency, and self-esteem. Spiritual combat is required to fight back. This is done through constant self-examination, prayer, and a willingness to use the Word of God to cleanse our heart.

> Who perceives his unintentional sins? Cleanse me from my hidden faults. Moreover, keep your servant from willful sins; do not let them rule me. Then I will be blameless and cleansed from blatant rebellion. May the words of my mouth and the meditation of my heart be acceptable to you, Lord, my rock and my Redeemer, Psalm 19:12–14.

Will we utilize God's revelation to:

- Discern our errors, 19:12?
- Prompt humility, 19:13?
- Seek forgiveness, 19:14a?
- Equip ourselves to seek to please God, 19:14b?

Will We Ask Hard Questions?

Our external actions may look good, especially if we define ourselves by what we do not do. Just because you may have never murdered anybody doesn't mean you are doing OK. Just because you have never committed adultery does not mean all is well between you and God. God's commands go far deeper into our minds and lives than just simply prohibiting the physical act of murder and adultery, Matthew 5:21–22; 27–28. What is going on inside your heart? Are you holding on to bitterness, malice, and a grudge? Are lustful thoughts occupying your mind? All may appear fine on the outside, but what is on the inside is what God is going to examine.

Christ criticized the Pharisees for putting the physical appearance of righteousness ahead of their responsibility to administer important spiritual aspects of God's law. In Matthew 23:23, He said:

> Woe to you, scribes and Pharisees, hypocrites! You pay a tenth of mint, dill, and cumin, and yet you have neglected the more important matters of the law—justice, mercy, and faithfulness. These things should have been done without neglecting the others, Matthew 23:23.

The Pharisees were obeying God's law in the letter, but they didn't ask themselves the hard questions to find out what they were missing. Instead of examining themselves and making the necessary corrections, their correction came forcefully from Jesus Christ and has been preserved for our instruction.

Self-examination isn't about making us feel good about ourselves or tearing ourselves down entirely. It's about identifying our faults so that we can change and become more like God. In short, examination is about asking the *hard questions*.[17]

---

17   Travers, Joshua. "Self-Examination: Asking the Hard Questions." Online. Retrieved 11/29/22 from https://members.cogwa.org/young-adult-blog/self-examination-asking-the-hard-questions/

Will We Call Sin What It Is?

Scripture is not shy about calling certain attitudes, thoughts, and behaviors "sinful." Sometimes, we are slow to examine ourselves because we do not call sin by its true name. The behavior of calling evil good and good evil, Isaiah 5:20, is still going on today. For example,

- In our giving, we might be robbing God, Malachi 3:8, while rationalizing that the economy is bad.
- In our behaviors, we might redefine sinful behavior as an "alternative lifestyle," 1 Corinthians 6:9–11.

No matter what we call it, our sin still breaks God's heart. We need to be honest with ourselves and with Him regarding our sinfulness.[18]

The Responsibility Lies with Us

Therefore, strengthen your tired hands and weakened knees, and make straight paths for your feet, so that what is lame may not be dislocated but healed instead, Hebrews 12:12–13.

We should examine ourselves and correct our own lives rather than have God correct us. The examined life is a biblical imperative.

Why is Self-Examination So Important?

You Are Not Above Falling

Perhaps the easiest reason is spelled out for us in 1 Corinthians 10:12: *So, whoever thinks he stands must be careful not to fall.* The possibility is real. The one who ignores his spiritual life will find it in danger.

18   Baker, John. "The Need for Self-Examination." Edgewood Church of Christ, Edgewood, TX. Online. Retrieved 11/29/22 from https://www.edgewoodcoc.org/the-need-for-self-examination/

Sometimes, we feel we are past the need to examine ourselves because we know all the basics and understand what God expects. This is a sure way to set oneself up for trouble.

God Examines Your Life, Whether You Do or Not

The fact is nobody lives an unexamined life. Even if you fail to do so, God will *and does.* The Lord *is the tester of hearts,* Proverbs 17:3. He sees all and knows all about us. Nobody was more insightful on this subject than the prophet Jeremiah, who said God *tests heart and mind,* Jeremiah 11:20; 20:12.

> I, the Lord, examine the mind, I test the heart to give to each according to his way, according to what his actions deserve, Jeremiah 17:10.

God does all this ultimately for our good—for rewards or for correction:

God's *eyes are on all the ways of the children of men in order to reward each person according to his ways and as the result of his actions,* Jeremiah 32:19.

The Bad Habits and Poor Patterns of Your Life Can Lead to Eternal Consequences

A failure to examine oneself leads to far-reaching eternal consequences:

> Don't be deceived: God is not mocked. For whatever a person sows he will also reap, because the one who sows to his flesh will reap destruction from the flesh, but the one who sows to the Spirit will reap eternal life from the Spirit, Galatians 6:7–8.

Too many people simply go through life unaware of how brief and uncertain it is. It is very easy to delude oneself into thinking that there is plenty of time to fix whatever is wrong and that it won't hurt if it is put off until a later time. If left unchecked, a lack of spiritual discipline will lead to eternal consequences which will not be reversed.

A Practical, Biblically Based Self-Exam for You

In Ephesians 4:13, Paul wrote about Christians pressing on for maturity and measuring themselves by the standard of Christ. With this, there will always be progress to be made. How can you measure yourself against the standard of Christ? One of the easiest ways is to look at the fruit of the Spirit, Galatians 5:22–23.

The fruit of the Spirit should be fully evident in every Christian's life. If something is missing in your life, that should be a warning that you have taken back control of some area of your life from the Spirit.
So here is the exam—a check of the fruit of the Spirit:

Ask These Questions

1. **Love**: Do I love others unconditionally? Do I withhold my love or forgiveness?
2. **Joy**: Am I able to rejoice in every circumstance? Can I give God thanks in all things?
3. **Peace**: Can I make it through a difficult circumstance without worry or depression?
4. **Patience/Longsuffering**: How often do I react impulsively instead of responding thoughtfully?
5. **Kindness**: Are my thoughts and words toward others graced with compassion?
6. **Goodness**: Am I willing to share what I have with others in need? Am I generous?
7. **Faithfulness**: Do I keep my word even when it is costly? Am I loyal to God and others?
8. **Gentleness**: Am I ever harsh, unyielding, or insistent on my interests instead of others'?

9. **Self-control**: Am I able to live out my priorities or am I subject to the desires of my flesh?[19]

Memorize

Commit Galatians 5:22–23 to memory.

Journal

Write down these nine traits of Christ's life and put them where you can review them daily. If you will do that faithfully, soon your heart and mind will respond immediately when the fruit of the Spirit has been overtaken by the work of the flesh in your life. You can instantly make whatever correction is needed: confess, repent, be filled with the Spirit, and move on.

You Are Not on Your Own

As you read this lesson, please do not think that all of this is up to you, and that's it. Don't forget that God has promised His help throughout the entire process. God has not set you up for failure; He equips you with success. Remember:

God has provided us with His word so that we know the definition of sin, 1 John 3:4.

God helps us to see the sin in our lives, Job 13:23; Romans 2:4, when we pray for correction, Jeremiah 10:23–24. One writer calls these risky prayers, pointing to the request of the Psalmist in Psalm 139:23–24. When you pray to ask God to search and try yourself, you better be ready to deal with sin because God will most certainly help you see what

---

19   Jeremiah, David. "Why Self-Examination is So Important." Online. Retrieved 11/30/22 from https://www.crosswalk.com/faith/spiritual-life/why-spiritual-self-examination-is-so-important.html

is lacking, 1 John 5:14–15. We need to be able to talk to God honestly and frankly about our sin. We also need to be able to ask God to help us see our sin. Risky prayers help us to look honestly at ourselves, and God answers prayers like that.[20]

When we seek to understand the way of righteousness, God helps us see the righteous conduct that must replace the sins, Matthew 5:6; Ephesians 4:24. Finally, God will help us to overcome our sins, 1 John 5:4, when we ask for His help while *struggling against sin*, Hebrews 12:4, and ourselves.

Never Forget Your Identity

It was Jeremiah who said,

> I know, Lord, that a person's way of life is not his own; no one who walks determines his own steps, Jeremiah 10:23.

You belong to God. As a good steward, live an examined life. Yield to the Holy Spirit moment by moment.

> Walk by the Spirit and you will certainly not carry out the desire of the flesh, Galatians 5:16.

> [You] have been crucified with Christ, and [you] no longer live, but Christ lives in [you]. The life [you] now live in the body, [you] live by faith in the Son of God, who loved [you] and gave himself for [you], Galatians 2:20.

---

20   Baker.

For Thought and Reflection

1. How do you define self-examination?

2. How can you fight back against your innate selfishness, i.e., your self-centeredness, desire for self-righteousness, lust for self-sufficiency, and craving for self-esteem?

3. What does Psalm 19:12–14 tell us about using the Word of God for self-examination?

4. How apt are we to gloss over sin by not identifying it properly? What can you do to not rationalize your sin?

5. Why is self-examination so important?

6. What is a "risky prayer?"

7. As we battle human pride and selfishness, why is it so important to remember our spiritual identity?

Lesson 4

Share Your Blessings

Introduction

G iving is the channel to blessing:

Give, and it will be given to you; a good measure—pressed down, shaken together, and running over—will be poured into your lap. For with the measure you use, it will be measured back to you, Luke 6:38.

Modern audiences may miss the imagery in this verse. Most Jews wore long robes that extended to their feet and would wear a belt around their waist. The bottom portion of the robe could be pulled up above the belt and formed into a large pocket for things to be carried. This is what Jesus is referring to when He says that blessings will be *poured into your lap.* The garment would literally be filled with grain.[21] The point that Jesus is trying to make is that God wants to fill our laps with abundant blessings to the point where they overflow.

Giving brings us reward from God. If you want blessing from God, if you want it poured out, overflowing, pressed down, shaken together, and running over, then give. You give and He gives back more.

Maybe this is why Paul quotes Jesus, who said *it is more blessed to give than receive,* Acts 20:35. What you give always brings you greater blessing than what you receive.

How much do we believe these promises? How easy is it to operate from the perspective of protecting everything and holding on to it? For some,

---

21   We also see this practice in Ruth 3:15.

self-preservation has led to stinginess. Will we operate by only what we can see, or will we move in faith and trust in God?

Just before Paul closes his letter to the Philippians, he writes out an incredible promise: *And my God will supply all your needs according to his riches in glory in Christ Jesus*, Philippians 4:19. God will meet every need. Because of Him, we have security in the promise of tomorrow. God will meet *every* need. We have nothing to fear for tomorrow. This is a foundational principle for the Christian life, and it should have a tremendous impact on our giving. Will we trust in God's promise?

But there is more. This is also a matter of obedience. Going back to our text in Luke 6:38, Jesus issues a command: *Give.* So, *not giving* is a sin. It is a sin against God because of a lack of trust. It is a sin against God because of a lack of obedience.

In and of themselves, Luke 6:38 and Acts 20:35 should be enough to create the type of response needed to influence us to give generously, unselfishly, and sacrificially.

Meeting the Needs of People

Benevolent needs were always present inside the early church. Widows, orphans, and poor people had needs that had to be met. Those who had been blessed with resources were instructed to share and thus store up treasure in heaven:

> Instruct those who are rich in the present age not to be arrogant or to set their hope on the uncertainty of wealth, but on God, who richly provides us with all things to enjoy. Instruct them to do what is good, to be rich in good works, to be generous and willing to share, storing up treasure for themselves as a good foundation for the coming age, so that they may take hold of what is truly life, 1 Timothy 6:17–19.

There were great needs to share … then … and now. Many among us have needs. God calls upon us to share. The principle is found throughout Scripture:

> "If there is a poor person among you, one of your brothers within any of your city gates in the land the Lord your God is giving you, do not be hardhearted or tightfisted toward your poor brother. Instead, you are to open your hand to him and freely loan him enough for whatever need he has. Be careful that there isn't this wicked thought in your heart, 'The seventh year, the year of canceling debts, is near,' and you are stingy toward your poor brother and give him nothing. He will cry out to the Lord against you, and you will be guilty. Give to him, and don't have a stingy heart when you give, and because of this the Lord your God will bless you in all your work and in everything you do. For there will never cease to be poor people in the land; that is why I am commanding you, 'Open your hand willingly to your poor and needy brother in your land,'" Deuteronomy 15:7–11.

Note the directive Israel had concerning the care of other poor Israelites:

- They were not to be hardhearted or *tightfisted.*
- They were to open their hand to him and *freely loan him enough for whatever need he has.*
- When you give, the Lord will *bless you in all your work and in everything you do.*

Give and God will bless. The Psalmist wrote:

> Happy is one who is considerate of the poor; the Lord will save him in a day of adversity. The Lord will keep him and preserve him; he will be blessed in the land. You will not give him over to the desire of his enemies. The Lord will sustain him on his sickbed; you will heal him on the bed where he lies, Psalm 41:1–3.

You should also take the time to discover the principles in Proverbs 14:31; 19:17; 22:2, 9.

A Greater Motive

When we see the early church giving to meet the needs of the poor, it wasn't just out of meeting someone's need ... it was to be generated by genuine love and concern. We must not forget the tremendous racial hatred and animosity of the first century. (Ours is not the only era of racial tension and hatred.) The hostility between Jews and Gentiles must not be forgotten. Overcoming it was a serious concern. When those in the church helped others, regardless of race or background, it was an expression of love and spiritual unity.

This is clearly seen with what happened with the early church of Acts 2. Although Gentiles were not yet present in the church, among the Jews were sharp divisions between groups of people—so much that they had no fellowship with each other. Now, because of Christ, all those barriers had been removed. What we see is a total commitment to share. The main thing we should get out of these verses is the amazing generosity practiced by the first Christians. Are we close to being as generous? The new converts of Acts 2 not only sacrificed their present reserves of cash and goods—but also their future—in acts that demonstrated sacrificial love.[22]

The Practice of Generosity

The ancient writer Chrysostom left us his thoughts on these verses:

> Observe the increase of piety. They cast away their riches, and rejoiced, and had great gladness, for greater were the riches they received without labour. None reproached, none envied, none grudged; no pride, no contempt was there. The poor man knew no shame, the rich no haughtiness.[23]

---

22   MacArthur, John F., Jr. *Acts*. MacArthur New Testament Commentary. Chicago: Moody Press, 1994., p. 87.

23   S. John Chrysostom. *The Homilies of S. John Chrysostom Archbishop of*

What we have with the practice of the early church is a beautiful expression of sacrificial love in its purest form. It was really nothing new to the Jews as there was a very strong tradition in the Old Testament of caring for the poor. Deuteronomy 26:12 prescribed:

> When you have finished paying all the tenth of your produce in the third year, the year of the tenth, you are to give it to the Levites, resident aliens, fatherless children, and widows, so that they may eat in your towns and be satisfied.

The principle of generosity denoted here remains the same for God's people of all time. While the New Testament makes this a matter of the heart and never goes into specific amounts that are required to give, we do read of two examples of the church going into action:

- Acts 2:45: *they distributed the proceeds to all, as any had need.*
- Acts 4:34–35: *for there was not a needy person among them because all those who owned lands or houses sold them, brought the proceeds of what was sold, and laid them at the apostles' feet. This was then distributed to each person as any had need.*

Later, the apostle John would write:

> If anyone has this world's goods and sees a fellow believer in need but withholds compassion from him—how does God's love reside in him? Little children, let us not love in word or speech, but in action and in truth, 1 John 3:17–18.

It has been said that "Christian fellowship is Christian caring, and Christian caring is Christian sharing."[24]

Constantinople, on the Acts of the Apostles: Parts I & II, Hom. I–LV. A Library of Fathers of the Holy Catholic Church. Oxford; London: John Henry Parker; F. and J. Rivington, 1851–1852, p. 108.

24 Stott, John R. W. *The Message of Acts: The Spirit, the Church & the World.* The Bible Speaks Today. Leicester, England; Downers Grove, IL: InterVarsity Press, 1994, p. 84.

Generosity Should Not Be Limited to
Only Our People

While the actions of the church body as a collective may be limited to helping saints from the treasury, no such limitations were placed on the individual. Let us be careful in our stand for what has been called "limited benevolence," that we do not ignore our individual responsibility to all:

> Therefore, as we have opportunity, let us work *for the good of all*, especially for those who belong to the household of faith, Galatians 6:10.

> See to it that no one repays evil for evil to anyone, but always pursue what is good for one another and *for all*, 1 Thessalonians 5:15.

> But If your *enemy* is hungry, feed him. If he is thirsty, give him something to drink. For in so doing you will be heaping fiery coals on his head, Romans 12:20.

Christians must never ignore the misery and destitution of the world. To meet the needs, we may need to be prepared to reorient our lifestyles so that we can maximize good deeds for all and to those who are part of the faith.

Conclusion

The church of today can and must be characterized by the same type of generosity ... demonstrated through sacrificial giving, donation of skill, and supply of time. We need to get out of ourselves and begin looking with a keen eye on how we can serve others. This is the type of church that will produce a credible witness that moves people to glorify our Father in heaven and cause us to have favor with all men.

For Thought and Reflection

1. What has God promised for those who give sacrificially?

2. Why do you think humans are so apt to rely on self-preservation?
   How does that impact the sharing of our resources?

3. Why is giving such an important matter? What did Jesus say about
   it?

4. In the church, what were those with resources instructed to do to
   help the needy among them?

5. With what kind of spirit are we to give?

6. Why should our generosity not only be limited to God's people?

Visit Orphans & Widows

My dear brothers and sisters, understand this: Everyone should
be quick to listen, slow to speak, and slow to anger, for human
anger does not accomplish God's righteousness. Therefore,
ridding yourselves of all moral filth and the evil that is so
prevalent, humbly receive the implanted word, which is able to
save your souls. But be doers of the word and not hearers only,
deceiving yourselves. Because if anyone is a hearer of the word
and not a doer, he is like someone looking at his own face in
a mirror. For he looks at himself, goes away, and immediately
forgets what kind of person he was. But the one who looks
intently into the perfect law of freedom and perseveres in it,
and is not a forgetful hearer but a doer who works—this person
will be blessed in what he does. If anyone thinks he is religious
without controlling his tongue, his religion is useless and he
deceives himself. Pure and undefiled religion before God the
Father is this: to look after orphans and widows in their distress
and to keep oneself unstained from the world, James 1:19–27.

Introduction

James 1:19–27 is an immensely practical section of Scripture that
serves as a strong warning against half-hearted Christianity that
listens and appears interested in divine truth but fails to
act on it. As we will see, the practice of Christianity is very practical
and demonstrates itself by applying what we know through external
obedience. It is not enough to hear the word. Until we have put the word
into practice, we have not truly listened, Matthew 7:24–27. A proper
response to Him will always be demonstrated by an obedient lifestyle
that proves we have heeded His teaching. Your spiritual life is to be
characterized by long-term obedience. You must *continue in the word*,
John 8:31.

James 1:19–27 contains a set of imperatives that must be followed. These are a natural result of the transforming power of the Spirit who works on the inside of us every day. He is working to ensure we have a greater and greater conformity to the image of Christ. The qualities James speaks of here should be growing into a regular part of our daily living.

There is a progression of thought that can be seen from verse 19 to the end of chapter 1. Each one of these main points lead into the next:

- 1:19—*be quick to listen,* **which means you must**…
- 1:21—*humbly receive the implanted word,* **which is proven by**:
- 1:22—(being) *a doer of the word,* **which is exemplified by**:
  - 1:26—(*controlling*) *your tongue.*
  - 1:27—(*looking*) *after orphans and widows in their distress.*
  - 1:27—(*keeping*) *yourself* unstained from the world.

Humbly receiving the implanted word, in 1:21, amplifies the command of being *quick to listen* in 1:19. Being *a doer of the word,* 1:22, spells out what it means to receive it. We have not "received" it when we only listen to it; we demonstrate we have "received" it in our day-by-day practice. The action word of 1:22 stresses continual, ongoing activity. The true reason for studying God's word is for our entire person to be changed *in every area* of life. This covers our whole self—mind, body, spirit, and emotions. In other words, obedience to the word becomes a matter of *who we are* vs. just something we do.

The principle of following through is seen throughout the New Testament. Grant Osborne's writing is an excellent summation:[25]

- Matthew 7:26 — Jesus says anyone who listens without obeying is a fool.
- Matthew 28:20 — the Great Commission also involves teaching those who come to Christ to *observe everything I have commanded you.*

---

25   Osborne, Grant R. *James: Verse by Verse.* Osborne New Testament Commentaries. Bellingham, WA: Lexham Press, 2019, p. 54.

- John 14:15-24 — loving Jesus will always result in doing what He says.
- Romans 2:13 — those who obey will be declared righteous.
- 2 Corinthians 10:5 — we must take every thought captive to obey Christ.
- 2 Timothy 3:15-16 — all Scripture has been given for teaching, rebuking, correcting, and training in righteousness.

James 1:23-24 vividly illustrates the preposterousness of listening without heeding by describing a person who looks in a mirror, sees things that need to be fixed, and then just walks away, *immediately forgetting* what they looked like.

Now, James 1:25 presents us with the application. God's word (*the perfect law of freedom*) serves as a spiritual mirror for us. How we are to look into the mirror of Scripture is very important. We are to look *intently,* i.e., with intensity. Looking reveals two things: our own sin *and* the sinless Savior and Lord. In other words, our careful study and meditation on the meaning of the text helps us see our sin for what it is and the *perfect* model to imitate. Then, we must *persevere in it.*

Will we allow it to impact our decisions?

Following through is what enables us to be *doers who work.* Are we eager to act on what we learn in the Word, working on improving our walk? Those who do so will be blessed. God's blessing comes from our obedience, both now and in the future. This principle is seen in the Old Testament:

> This book of instruction must not depart from your mouth; you are to meditate on it day and night so that you may carefully observe everything written in it. For then you will prosper and succeed in whatever you do, Joshua 1:8.

In Romans 2:10, Paul speaks of *glory, honor, and peace for everyone who does what is good.* When we follow through in compliance to the will of God, His blessings will shower down upon us.

What blessings have you received in this life because of your obedience to the Word of God?

Pure and Undefiled Religion

What It Is Not

James 1:26-27 completes the progression that began with the command to be *quick to listen* in 1:19. Verse 26 describes what true religion is not. A person who observes all the outward aspects of *religion but* cannot bridle his tongue reveals that the Word has yet to penetrate his heart. *For the mouth speaks from the overflow of the heart,* Matthew 12:34. A person who fails to control his tongue is likely to have spiritual heart disease. People can gossip, speak angry words, or malign the character of others. James insists that the person whose life is characterized by these habits has a worthless religion. Pretty serious stuff.

An Internet search reveals that the average person speaks around 7000 words each day, with many speaking much more than that, some estimates being as high as 13,000 words. This is enough to produce a 40-50 page book, which over the course of a year would accumulate to as many as 18,250 pages! Could you imagine a series of books being written containing the things you speak? How much of what you talk about glorifies God?

What It Is

While certainly not a comprehensive listing, James identifies the practice of true religious acts that are acceptable before God:

- Looking after orphans and widows in their distress, 1:27a.
- Keeping ourselves unstained from the world, 1:27b.

True religion involves practical behavior. For example, Paul speaks of the need to pursue righteousness, faith, love, and peace, 2 Timothy 2:22.

Peter wrote about showing *sincere brotherly love for each other, from a pure heart love one another constantly*, 1 Peter 1:22. Religious observance without the practice of these things is nothing. It is empty, meaningless, and just a waste of time.

Looking After Orphans and Widows

Many of us have heard and read a great deal of preaching and teaching on James 1:27, but mainly from the perspective of what it does not teach. We may have focused so much on the negative that, in many cases, we may simply wind up doing nothing, *all the while feeling justified about our inaction!* This totally goes against the spirit inside the context of this part of James.

To "look after" or "visit" orphans and widows comes from the same root word[26] used to describe the actions of an "overseer" or "bishop." So, this is something more than a Sunday afternoon visit ... *looking after* orphans and widows involves exercising care and oversight on their behalf. We are to "take care of or see to" their needs. It involves the implication of continuous responsibility.[27] Another writer says it involves coming to their aid and paying close attention to their needs.[28]

Widows and orphans were often the neediest in first-century society. The loss of a husband in ancient times was usually a tragic occurrence both socially and economically. Among her friends and acquaintances, the widow would have quickly become associated with a person dwelling in extreme poverty, living on a marginal existence. While today Americans have a built-in safety net of social security survivor benefits, life insurance, and government assistance, none of that was available for

---

26   See Acts 20:28; Philippians 1:1; 1 Timothy 3:2; Titus 1:7; and 1 Peter 2:25.

27   Louw, Johannes P., and Eugene Albert Nida. *Greek-English Lexicon of the New Testament: Based on Semantic Domains.* New York: United Bible Societies, 1996, Vol. 1, p. 462.

28   This is the way God "visited" His people, delivering them from oppression, Genesis 50:24; Exodus 3:16; Ruth 1:6. See Osborne, p. 60.

them during that time. Similar conditions to those in the first century still exist in many third-world countries today. During the first century, widows were especially vulnerable as they had no male protector. If there was an inheritance, it went to the firstborn son. Care for the widow fell back on her parental family, who often ignored her needs.

Orphans were also destitute because they had no family. Typically, those in society cared little for their plight. Widows and orphans would have been in the deepest need of those inside the church.

Taking Scripture as a whole, we see God's special awareness and concern for orphans and widows, commanding His people to demonstrate love and care for them. *You must not mistreat any widow or fatherless child,* Exodus 22:22. *The one who denies justice to a resident alien, a fatherless child, or a widow is cursed,* Deuteronomy 27:19. Here are a few other notable Old Testament passages. We must defend their rights and never oppress them:

- Isaiah 1:17: *Learn to do what is good. Pursue justice. Correct the oppressor. Defend the rights of the fatherless. Plead the widow's cause.*
- Jeremiah 7:6: *if you no longer oppress the resident alien, the fatherless, and the widow and no longer shed innocent blood in this place or follow other gods, bringing harm on yourselves,*
- Ezekiel 22:7: *Father and mother are treated with contempt, and the resident alien is exploited within you. The fatherless and widow are oppressed in you.*
- Zechariah 7:10: *Do not oppress the widow or the fatherless, the resident alien or the poor, and do not plot evil in your hearts against one another.*

Loving, Selfless Service

Pure and undefiled religion in the sight of God is to serve others with love and compassion. Paul commanded that Christians *support widows who are genuinely in need,* 1 Timothy 5:3. If they need financial assistance or have any other concerns, those are to be met. This is undoubtedly an application of John's teaching:

- 1 John 2:10-11: *The one who loves his brother or sister remains in the light, and there is no cause for stumbling in him. But the one who hates his brother or sister is in the darkness, walks in the darkness, and doesn't know where he is going, because the darkness has blinded his eyes.*
- 1 John 3:10b-11: *Whoever does not do what is right is not of God, especially the one who does not love his brother or sister. For this is the message you have heard from the beginning: We should love one another...*
- 1 John 3:14: *We know that we have passed from death to life because we love our brothers and sisters. The one who does not love remains in death.*
- 1 John 3:16-18: *This is how we have come to know love: He laid down his life for us. We should also lay down our lives for our brothers and sisters. If anyone has this world's goods and sees a fellow believer in need but withholds compassion from him—how does God's love reside in him? Little children, let us not love in word or speech, but in action and in truth.*

The Most Visible Trait of Our Salvation

By this all will know you are my disciples, if you have love for one another, John 13:35. True Christianity is demonstrated by how we love and care for those in need. All persons. Not just those we prefer or who are like us or are in our close circle of friends and acquaintances. It should be our desire to help, strengthen, and encourage them. We help orphans and widows and people in distress.

Who Can You Serve?

Today would be a great day to go through your church directory and make a listing of all the widows and widowers. First, you might be amazed at how many there are. Now, pick out one or two. How can you pray for them in a specific way? Would they appreciate a card, phone call, or even better ... a visit? Could you prepare them a meal? What might be an event that you could invite them to go along with you? The possibilities of what you can do to serve are as plentiful as they can be.

While many congregations today have no orphans among them, there are several good organizations connected with brethren that are committed to meeting their needs. They could always use your donations. Pick one of these and find a way to help. You'll be glad you did.

Pure and genuine love always expresses itself in word and deed.

For Thought and Reflection

1. How can we look into the mirror of Scripture more effectively and actively persevere in making the appropriate changes?

2. What blessings have you received in this life because of your obedience to the Word?

3. How much of what you talk about glorifies God?

4. Who are some widows/widowers you can serve in your congregation?

5. What are some needs they have that you can meet?

6. What are some organizations or adoption agencies that help provide for orphans that you can support?

Lesson 6

Overflowing with Gratitude

Introduction

One of the basic themes of the book of Colossians is thankfulness. Paul continually reminds his readers of their need for it.

- He speaks of his desire for them to express it as they reflect on God's great work of salvation in them and among them, 1:12–14.
- He speaks of how our *overflowing with gratitude* is the natural result of being connected (or rooted) to our life source: Jesus, 2:6–7.
- Again, in 3:15–16, he talks of being thankful and having gratitude in one's heart.
- And finally, in 4:2, he tells us to *stay alert in prayer with thanksgiving.*

Why so much emphasis on thankfulness?

Think of how it can serve as a protection against the lying attacks of Satan. When we focus on how good God is, how gracious He is, and how caring He is, it reinforces our resolve to remain faithful.

For what should we be thankful? An examination of Colossians reveals five things.

Gratitude for Salvation

Giving thanks to the Father, who has enabled you to share in the saints' inheritance in the light. He has rescued us from the domain of darkness and transferred us into the kingdom of the

Son he loves. In him we have redemption, the forgiveness of sins, Colossians 1:12–14.

In These Verses We Find Four Things to Praise God for

First, **he has *enabled you to share in the saints' inheritance in the light*, 1:12**. At one time, you were an enemy of God, a sinner separated from Him. By enabling you, God has empowered you or helped make you complete. You, who were once unworthy, have been made worthy of receiving the saints' inheritance. That is simply incredible!

Next, **he has liberated you by rescuing you from *the domain of darkness*, 1:13**. When you were baptized, God transferred you to the place where Satan can't dwell. The *transfer* that took place describes a change in geography, place, or residence. You have been totally removed from Satanic darkness and placed where Jesus reigns.

Some have linked 1:13 to what happened with the Hebrew people in Exodus 6:6–8. God rescued them from oppression, brutality, and slavery. Even this far back in history, we see God delivering, redeeming, and bringing His people to the place He desires.

Third, **he has redeemed you through Christ, 1:14a**. You, as a sinner, were a slave to your sin. Jesus paid the price for your sin at the cross, changing your condition. You are no longer a slave to sin, but now you are bound to God, Romans 6:22. Your allegiance to Him *results in sanctification—and the outcome is eternal life!* Praise God!

Finally, **he has forgiven and forgotten your debt of sin, 1:14b**. You, as a sinner, had piled up an unpayable debt before God. You are no longer under condemnation, Romans 8:1.

- All the sins of your past have been forgiven. Your sins have been sent away *as far as the east is from the west*, Psalm 103:12. Your sins *have been cast into the depths of the sea*, Micah 7:19.

- All your present sins are forgiven. You *stand* in grace, Romans 5:1–2.
- All the sins of your future are forgiven if one remains faithful, Ephesians 1:9–14. Jesus ever lives to make intercession for you, Hebrews 7:25.

By your obedient response to Christ, you have been brought in on God's plan of restoration, reconciliation, and mercy. If you remain steadfast in your commitment, your salvation rests on the continuous work of God, who is more than committed to seeing His work completed in you. When you walk daily with God, your salvation is never precarious.

> I am sure of this, that he who started a good work in you will carry it on to completion until the day of Christ Jesus. Therefore, my dear friends, just as you have always obeyed, so now, not only in my presence but even more in my absence, work out your own salvation with fear and trembling. For it is God who is working in you both to will and to work according to his good purpose, Philippians 1:6; 2:12–13.

What a tremendous reason to have a heart filled with gratitude! When we think of where we were and where we were headed, and now, because of the great love and care of our God, all that has changed. The praise should pour out of us!

Gratitude for Growth and Progress

> So then, just as you have received Christ Jesus as Lord, continue to walk in him, being rooted and built up in him and established in the faith, just as you were taught, and overflowing with gratitude, Colossians 2:6–7.

Some have suggested that 2:6a is hinting at the significance of baptism and the commitment made in that action.[29] It certainly doesn't add to

---

29   Wright, N.T. *Colossians and Philemon: An Introduction and Commentary.* Vol. 12 of *Tyndale New Testament Commentaries.* Downers Grove, IL: InterVarsity Press, 1986, 103.

the context because a few sentences later, v. 12 specifically, Paul focuses on it in greater detail. On the occasion of their salvation, the Colossian Christians would have confessed their belief in Jesus as Christ and voiced their desire for Him to be their Lord. Think back to that day and compare who you were then and who you are now. It is important to remember and meditate on the great things Christ has done for you. You are not the same person you were then, and it is by His power that that is so. What a tremendous thing to be grateful for!

We should also be thankful for the stability Christ provides. *We have been rooted and built up in him and established in the faith,* 2:7. There is a combination of imagery in this verse. Paul is saying we have sunk our roots into Christ. This happened at baptism. And every moment afterward, He continually supplies our spiritual life. He is your spiritual life source, providing spiritual nourishment, growth, and fruit. As you walk in Him, you are continually being *built up in Him and established in the faith.* God is the one who provides us with a firm foundation for our faith to grow into a healthy spiritual life. Into what has God grounded us?

- Our understanding that He is in control, Romans 8:28; Psalm 42:6–7.
- Our realization that the trials of life have purpose, James 1:12.
- Our increasing dependence on God to supply all our needs, James 1:5, 17–18; Philippians 4:19.
- Our growing likeness of Christ, our daily transformation to where we respond to life as He would, not the way our old self would, Colossians 3:10–11.

When we contemplate these things, we can't help but overflow with gratitude!

Fellowship with Christ and His Church

And let the peace of Christ, to which you were also called in one body, rule your hearts. And be thankful, Colossians 3:15.

The peace Paul mentions at the beginning of this verse is both a state and an experience. You should be very thankful for the peace you now enjoy with our Lord. Once you were an enemy, Romans 5:10, but you have been reconciled, Colossians 1:19–20. You are now "in agreement" with Him. You are now inside a relationship with Him. This leads to an experience of peace, inner rest, and calm. As you meditate on this, we realize that the King of the universe is assisting in and directing our life. He calls the shots and will never lead us off the path.

Along with this, you are never alone. You have been *called into one body*. You now get to do life together with other believers who help hold you up. It is so important to see the church in a positive light, seeing and appreciating our essential connection with our spiritual family. We need to see the value of the local church.

The *thankfulness* described in this verse is the defining characteristic of the believer. Ingratitude defines the unbeliever, not the child of God, Romans 1:21.

Opportunities to Serve

And whatever you do, in word or in deed, do everything in the name of the Lord Jesus, giving thanks to God the Father through him, Colossians 3:17.

This verse is written in the context of our personal relationship with people inside the body. Whatever we do in service to others becomes an opportunity to bring glory to the name of God. This is something that should become a pleasure for us. As we serve others, we are filled with joy when they are filled with joy.

Colossians 3:17 completes the thought Paul began in 2:6 ... *continue to walk in Him.* We represent Jesus in everything we do. He empowers us to do good to others. Remember, He is our life source and gives us the spiritual energy to accomplish His work. We comply with the direction of the Spirit with an attitude of thanks. God has done so much for us by placing people in our lives so we can serve them.

Answered Prayer

> Devote yourselves to prayer; stay alert in it with thanksgiving, Colossians 4:2.

This verse describes three aspects of our prayer life.

First, **we make intercessions to our God**. This is the action of casting all our cares upon the God who cares for us, 1 Peter 5:7.

Next, **we watch for His answer**. We *stay alert in it.* In other words, we live in anticipation of how God will answer our prayers. We trust God and will not go around filled with anxiousness and worry. So, we wait and watch as to how God will move.

Finally, **we are filled with thanksgiving when He answers**. We do so, however He answers, with the spirit of gratitude and thankfulness. God is with us. God provides for us. He forgives us. He promises an inheritance and works things out for us as we move forward on our spiritual journey. Truly, God is an amazing God!

Conclusion

God is so good. We all have so much to be thankful for! No one can receive anything unless it has been given to him from heaven, John 3:27. God has you. He has your back. He has saved you. He is filling your life with blessings. He is leading you home. For what more could you ask?

For Thought and Reflection

1. What makes you most thankful about your salvation? Why?

2. Since your baptism, what are you most thankful for in your transformation? Where do you think God has accomplished the most in changing who you are? How does this make you grateful?

3. Why is it so important to see the church in a positive light?

4. What is the defining characteristic of the believer?

5. What is so joyful about serving others?

6. Thinking about the prayers you have prayed, how has God answered them? What are you thankful for?

Lesson 7

Weeping/Rejoicing
with Brethren

Introduction

In Paul's writings to the churches at Rome and Corinth, two passages stand out:

Rejoice with those who rejoice, weep with those who weep, Romans 12:15.

If one member suffers, all suffer together; if one member is honored, all rejoice together, 1 Corinthians 12:26.

From Paul's writings, we learn Christians should have a unique care for one another. When we discuss fellowship, there is a certain inherent unity and togetherness. Following through on what is written in these two passages provides powerful evidence of our fellowship together.

What does it mean to rejoice together?

A Look at the Context of Romans 12

Romans 12 begins the application section of the book. While the first 11 chapters are primarily doctrinal, looking at the basis of our salvation and the assurance of it, the final 5 demonstrate the result of that salvation: a changed life.

Romans 12:9 is speaking to the individual Christian. Practical Christian living begins with simple priorities:

- Honest love, 12:9a
- Hating evil, 12:9b
- A commitment to what is right, 12:9c

In Romans 12:10–13, the focus widens to the Christian family. We are each called to:

- Love one another with brotherly affection, 12:10a.
- Seek, above all, to honor other Christians, rather than be honored yourself, 12:10b.
- Serve others with enthusiastic, whole-hearted, zealous, obedient, and diligent care, 12:11.
- Endure trials, our own **and** the trials of others. During those times, we are to rejoice, be patient, and be constant in prayer, 12:12.
- See to the needs of others, 12:13.

In Romans 12:14–16 we look outside the body and think of all people. These verses challenge us on how we live in relationship with every person. In 12:14, Paul begins with the worst of people: *those who persecute you.* How should we respond? *With a blessing.* Again, this is a general statement. *Anyone who persecutes you, you bless.* This teaching is distinctively Christian. The world does not respond to mistreatment or persecution with love. But here, we are instructed to "pursue the one who treats us with evil intentions with the purpose of honoring and blessing them."

Finally, in Romans 12:17–21—the focus goes all the way to our enemies. We are to always *maintain our honor,* 12:17; *live peaceably with all,* 12:18; and to *never avenge ourselves,* 12:19–20. This is all so we can overcome evil, not be overcome by it.

Rejoicing with Those Who Rejoice

In explaining the context, I purposely left out comments on 12:15–16. Now that we understand the background and Paul's purpose behind these writings, we'll look at these two verses in depth.

Rejoice with Those Who Rejoice, Weep with Those Who Weep

This is the natural result of true love and humility. It is the application of loving like Jesus. It is not always easy to get in touch with the emotions of others. Inherent in 12:15 are the concepts of:

- **Compassion** which means *suffering with.*
- **Empathy** which is *the ability to identify with and experience the feelings and dispositions of others.*[30]

When we rejoice with others, we share their joys, triumphs, and successes. This can be a challenge. For example, seeing others succeed where we have failed can lead to envy, jealousy, and resentment. So, following through on what Paul is calling for in this verse requires the total absence of these things. MacArthur says it is distinctively Christian to rejoice at someone else's prosperity.[31] Think about it this way: *What do the worldly do?* **Whoever mocks the poor insults his Maker; he who is glad at calamity will not go unpunished**, Proverbs 17:5.

How Do We Accomplish This?

The key is found in 12:16: *live in harmony with each other.* The NASB says *be of the same mind toward each other.* The admonition is to think

---

30   Cottrell, Jack. *Romans.* Vol. 2. The College Press NIV Commentary. Joplin, MO: College Press Pub. Co., 1996.

31   MacArthur, John. *Romans.* logos.com. Bellingham, WA, 1991.

about everyone the same. Later in Romans, Paul would write: *May the God of endurance and encouragement grant you to live in such harmony with one another, in accord with Christ Jesus,* Romans 15.5. Think also of the teaching found in Philippians 1:27 and 2:2–4.

When Paul wrote 1 Corinthians 1:10, the emphasis was not focused as much on doctrinal correctness as it was on eliminating social cliques and social strata. Christians are to *be united in the same mind and the same judgment.*

Now, back to our passage in 12:16. Paul gives two suggestions on how to live together in harmony:

Don't Be Haughty but Associate with the Lowly

We're not to concentrate on high things but to associate or *be carried away with* that which is lowly.[32] This doesn't mean that we never associate with those who are high up—it's just that we don't pursue high status or concentrate on "high" things.

Never Be Wise in Your Own Sight

In other words, don't be satisfied that everything begins and ends with you. Lean not on your own understanding, Proverbs 3:5.

Weeping with Those Who Weep

When compared with the *rejoicing* that is mentioned in the first part of the verse, the *weeping* may appear to be easier. But it does require deliberate effort. It is not always easy for us to involve ourselves in the distress of others. But throughout both Old and New Testament periods, it is something that God's people have been called upon to do.

---

32   Kittel, Gerhard, Geoffrey W. Bromiley, and Gerhard Friedrich, eds. "Εὐπροσωπέω." *Theological Dictionary of the New Testament.* Grand Rapids, MI: Eerdmans, 1964–.

Why This Can Be Difficult

It is easy to be indifferent to the troubles and sorrows of others, especially when we are dealing with our own. Our mind might say, *I have enough of my own problems, why get involved with someone else's?* Or, *I can barely cope with my situation, how could I possibly offer something of value to someone else?*

Also, we need to guard against the tendency to gloat when people's sufferings result from their own carelessness and sin. We must resist the urge to say, "they get what they deserve."

Job's Friends

Job's trouble came upon him suddenly and with no expectation. Not only did he lose all his material possessions and offspring (Job 1), but he also lost his health (Job 2:1–10). Upon hearing this, Eliphaz, Bildad, and Zophar came to comfort him. We read:

> Now when Job's three friends heard of all this evil that had come upon him, they came each from his own place, Eliphaz the Temanite, Bildad the Shuhite, and Zophar the Naamathite. They made an appointment together to come to show him sympathy and comfort him. And when they saw him from a distance, they did not recognize him. And they raised their voices and wept, and they tore their robes and sprinkled dust on their heads toward heaven. And they sat with him on the ground seven days and seven nights, and no one spoke a word to him, for they saw that his suffering was very great, Job 2:11–13.

What is said here is very moving. Just read the words slowly and let them sink in:

- Job's condition was so bad *they did not recognize him.*
- His suffering was *very great.*

- When they saw him, Eliphaz, Bildad, and Zophar *raised their voices and wept, and they tore their robes and sprinkled dust on their heads …*
- They *sat with Job on the ground, … and no one spoke a word to him.*

Sometimes, all you can do is be there. The grief is so overwhelming, astonishing, and stupefying that no words are adequate. In these situations, there is a *reverential awe* with which we approach the sufferer and a *tender caution* with which we address them.[33] It is almost as if any words spoken would be out of place.

Other Biblical Examples

Two additional examples stand out where Biblical characters exhibited deep and tender compassion toward others who were not necessarily fellow followers of God. One is in Psalm 35:13–14: *But I, when they were sick—I wore sackcloth; I afflicted myself with fasting; I prayed with head bowed on my chest. I went about as though I grieved for my friend or my brother; as one who laments his mother, I bowed down in mourning.* Here, David is seeking God's justice against those who have aligned against him. But notice his actions in previous times. See his empathy and compassion for others as they were struggling.

Another example is in the gospels during Jesus' teaching in Luke 10:30–37. In this case, the Samaritan man exhibited great empathy as he cared for the man who had been beaten, robbed, and left for dead on the side of the road. He made the other man's problems his own. He sacrificed his own safety, time, and resources to make sure the man received the proper care during a very difficult time.

---

33 Simeon, Charles. *Horae Homileticae: Romans.* Vol. 15. London: Holdsworth and Ball, 1833.

How Empathy Benefits

The Giver

When we are empathetic toward others, it can inspire within us a sense of gratitude toward God for His personal sustaining and care as well as remind us of our total dependence on Him. It also forces us to recognize that our own personal troubles may be much lighter when compared to those around us.

The Receiver

Our care and concern take some of the weight of the sorrow away. It can serve as a balm to heal the wound suffering creates. It also can help divert their mind from only focusing on their troubles to *reciprocal affection*[34] and an attitude of gratitude to a very gracious God.

The Church

When these attitudes, care, and concern are displayed in full force and activity, the cause of Christ is greatly promoted. The beauty and excellence of Christianity is seen. Think of how those who beheld Jesus at the tomb of Lazarus were struck with His empathy:

> When Jesus saw her weeping, and the Jews who had come with her also weeping, he was deeply moved in his spirit and greatly troubled. And he said, "Where have you laid him?" They said to him, "Lord, come and see." Jesus wept. So the Jews said, "See how he loved him!", John 11:33–36.

When persons behold Christians participating with others freely in their joys and sorrows, they too will say, "Behold how these Christians

---

34   Simeon.

love one another; yea, and not one another only, but all around them, strangers and enemies, as well as friends!"[35] The prevalence of this disposition goes further to silence those who speak negatively about Christianity, and wins more souls, than all the arguments of doctrinal knowledge. In other words, we can speak to them in a language which they cannot but understand and feel.

Conclusion

Consider the following passages:

- *Finally, all of you, have unity of mind, sympathy, brotherly love, a tender heart, and a humble mind, 1 Peter 3:8.* We need to share the same passions. Our desire to be like our Savior and Father should imprint a mutuality of concern for one another because of our common fervency for God's redemptive rule. We need to stand together to survive.[36]
- *Remember those who are in prison, as though in prison with them, and those who are mistreated, since you also are in the body," Hebrews 13:3.*
- *Let no one seek his own good, but the good of his neighbor, 1 Corinthians 10:24.*
- *If one member suffers, all suffer together; if one member is honored, all rejoice together, 1 Corinthians 12:26.*

---

35   Simeon.

36   Garrett, Linda. "Love Divided Against Itself?" *Bible Study Magazine.* Page 6. Volume 9, No. 5, July/August 2017.

For Thought and Reflection

1. When you read Romans 12:15 and 1 Corinthians 12:26, how do these verses affect you? Are you doing a good job applying these passages? If not, what is holding you back?

2. How are compassion and empathy defined?

3. Do you think weeping with those who weep can be more difficult than rejoicing with those who rejoice? Or vice versa? Why?

4. How can the Good Samaritan inspire you to be more empathetic?

5. What are some things you can do to grow in your empathy toward others?

6. When we help people through their problems, what does it remind us about our problems?

7. Where would you be today without the care and support of others who stood with you during dark times?

Lesson 8

Be Angry and Sin Not

Be angry and do not sin. Don't let the sun go down on your anger, and don't give the devil an opportunity, Ephesians 4:26–27.

Introduction

Can you imagine what would happen if everyone learned how to put away sinful anger? Child abuse and divorce would go away. Murder, terrorism, and war would halt. And, amazingly, many health problems would clear up. It is believed that anger can harm a person's heart just as much as smoking and high blood pressure. Some have even gone as far as to say that it is a leading indicator of a person acquiring heart disease.

It is not by accident that Paul addresses the imperative of casting off the old man and putting on the new just before he teaches about the problem of anger.

> to take off your former way of life, the old self that is corrupted by deceitful desires, to be renewed in the spirit of your minds, and to put on the new self, the one created according to God's likeness in righteousness and purity of the truth, Ephesians 4:22-24.

See the contrasts. There is an *old self* and a *new self*. One is to be *taken off;* the other is to be *put on.* One is *corrupted;* the other is *created.* The old self is connected to *deceitful desires;* the new self is connected to *righteousness and purity of the truth.*

God has recreated you, being made alive by the Spirit as an act of grace, Ephesians 2:5. You have been created as God's masterpiece, created for good works, Ephesians 2:10. Paul goes on to say that we are expected to walk in those good works. Fundamental to this "walking" is the putting on of the new self. We must *act it out* by making it visible in our attitudes and behavior.[37]

The emphasis in Ephesians 4:23-24 is that God has created in you a new heart, one that is like His in *righteousness and purity*. If your heart has been purified, it will surely reflect itself in your actions. *A good tree produces good fruit*, Matthew 7;17. All our external actions reflect the change that has taken place on the inside. Understanding what Paul communicates in these verses is key to finding success in the fight against uncontrolled anger. Verses 26-27 are a specific application of one of the ways we are to put on the new man. Here we find two points regarding anger:

There Is a Right Time to Be Angry

Be angry and not sin. This is taken from Psalm 4:4. Of the four problems listed in 4:25-29 (lying, anger, stealing, and foul language), only anger is mentioned as having a time that is appropriate. It is a God-given emotion that can be proper and even essential. Having and expressing emotion and feelings is not a matter of sin. However, we must guard what we do with those feelings, how we express them, and how they impact others. Some expressions of anger are clearly wrong:

> Let all bitterness, anger and wrath, shouting and slander be removed from you, along with all malice, Ephesians 4:31.

---

37   Piper, John. *Sermons from John Piper (1980–1989)*. Minneapolis, MN: Desiring God, 2007.

Acceptable Anger

This type of anger arises from deep, settled convictions regarding the honor of God. We should be angry at injustice, immorality, and ungodliness. This is the type of anger David spoke of in Psalm 69:9: *zeal for your house has consumed me, and the insults of those who insult you have fallen on me.* This kind of love is unselfish. It is based on love for God and concern for others.

It is something that should rise slowly from within. James 1:19-20 teaches us to be *slow to anger.* We are to be slow to anger so that we will be able to rule our spirit and consider the situation with care. Unrestrained anger that is allowed to rise quickly will never bring glory to God and magnify the righteous character we are to possess. Unacceptable, sinful anger is a boiling-over rage or inward seething resentment. It is buried in self-defense and is often self-serving. It is undisciplined and vindictive. Injured pride, envy, and spite fuel sinful anger.

Connected with Grief

Acceptable anger is also connected closely to grief. That is, we direct our emotions against the *sin* but also connect it with grief for the *sinner.* We must never forget there is a person behind the situation … a person who has been created in the image of God. Many times, it is a brother or sister in Christ. When we get in these situations, we need to move with hope for reconciliation and not just write the person off.

If possible, as far as it depends on you, live at peace with everyone, Romans 12:18.

Deal with Your Anger Quickly

Don't let the sun go down on your anger..., 4:26b. If you hang on to anger, it can quickly turn into bitterness and manifest itself in wrath. It has been said that righteous anger very easily becomes perverted and soured and is turned against those we love. Passionate feelings against others and their actions are not to be harbored for very long. In the Torah, sunset was the time limit for paying a worker his wages, Deuteronomy 24:15. Some feel Paul has picked up on this principle and applied it here ... saying there is danger in holding on to anger too long.

This is what Paul means in 4:27: *don't give the devil an opportunity.* What can start out as righteous, healthy anger can be held on to or even nursed. Then, it becomes personal and a matter of personal pride. This is the type of anger that has been described as "evil in itself, and dishonorable to God; being the vomit of a proud heart and unmeekened spirit."[38]

It is this type of anger that makes us worse than the one who offended us and turns them into the victim!

This quote by Frederick Buechner is found in Kent Hughes'[39] work:

> Of the seven deadly sins, anger is possibly the most fun. To lick your wounds, to smack your lips over grievances long past, to roll over your tongue the prospect of bitter confrontation still to come, to savor to the last toothsome morsel both the pain you are given and the pain you are giving back; in many ways it is a feast fit for a king. The chief drawback is that what you are wolfing down is yourself. The skeleton at the feast is you.

---

38   Boston, Thomas. *The Complete Works of the Late Rev. Thomas Boston*, Volume 4, ed. Samuel McMillan (Wheaton, IL: Richard Owen Roberts, 1980), p. 357.

39   Hughes, R. Kent. *Ephesians: The Mystery of the Body of Christ*. Preaching the Word. Wheaton, IL: Crossway Books, 1990, p. 151.

You Can Control Your Anger

We are expected to overcome our sins. The power to do so is given to us by the Spirit. No exceptions are made for those who are born with a short fuse or have fallen prey as a victim. He simply says:

> Let all bitterness, anger and wrath, shouting and slander be removed from you, along with all malice, Ephesians 4:31.

This is not the only passage in the New or Old Testament that teaches us to learn to control our anger:

- Proverbs 12:18: *There is one who speaks rashly, like a piercing sword; but the tongue of the wise brings healing.*
- Proverbs 14:16–17: *A wise person is cautious and turns from evil, but a fool is easily angered and is careless. A quick-tempered person acts foolishly, and one who schemes is hated.*
- Proverbs 15:1: *A gentle answer turns away anger, but a harsh word stirs up wrath.*
- Proverbs 15:18: *A hot-tempered person stirs up conflict, but one slow to anger calms strife.*
- Proverbs 17:14: *To start a conflict is to release a flood; stop the dispute before it breaks out.*
- Proverbs 19:11: *A person's insight gives him patience, and his virtue is to overlook an offense.*
- Genesis 4:7: Cain was told he must master his sin. *If you do what is right, won't you be accepted? But if you do not do what is right, sin is crouching at the door. Its desire is for you, but you must rule over it."*

Scripture tells us that we are never expected to do what we cannot possibly do, 1 Corinthians 10:13. You can do this. You must learn to replace the works of the flesh with the fruit of the Spirit. This is accomplished by walking by the Spirit. When we do so, we will not carry out the desires of the flesh, Galatians 5:16.

This is a process that is learned over time. It requires constant attention. When we feel sinful anger arising, we must learn to yield to the Spirit and rely on His strength.

Will We Submit to the Spirit's Direction?

Our own experience typically proves that we can control our anger if we want to do so. Every one of us has controlled our anger—instantly turned it off—*when we wanted to*. Maybe you have been in a heated argument with someone … then the phone rings. You answer and say, "Hey there, it's so good to hear from you! How are you doing?" In that instant, you are controlling your anger. The same is true when your employer says something that upsets you greatly, but you keep your composure because you value your job. You can do this. You simply need to choose to do it consistently.

For Thought and Reflection

1. What has been the most difficult part for you in controlling your anger? How can you deal with it?

2. Why is it important to understand Paul does not say all anger is sin? At what point do our angry feelings become sin?

3. Why is it important to handle our anger in a timely manner?

4. Can we control our feelings? Do you think Paul's command to put it away is simplistic? Why/Why not?

5. Why should our righteous anger be connected to grief?

6. Who is righteous anger always focused upon? What typically happens if it is focused on us?

Lesson 9

Submit to One Another

And don't get drunk with wine, which leads to reckless living, but be filled by the Spirit: speaking to one another in psalms, hymns, and spiritual songs, singing and making music with your heart to the Lord, giving thanks always for everything to God the Father in the name of our Lord Jesus Christ, submitting to one another in the fear of Christ, Ephesians 5:18–21.

Introduction

Have you ever wondered why Paul would contrast drunkenness with being filled with the Spirit? Those reading in Ephesus would have drawn an immediate connection. Ephesus was home to the temple of Dionysius, the god associated with drunken orgies and frenzied behavior. The backgrounds of many of the Christians in the church there might have been associated in this activity. Paganism had been their life. Now, in contrast to that, Paul's emphasis here is not just the negative command of avoiding drunkenness, but rather it is being filled with the Spirit. Paul describes this as a continuous, ongoing, daily pursuit. Whatever we do in terms of the Christian life, it must flow from a life controlled by the Spirit. This will impact every relationship we have in life.

What Happens When I am Filled with the Spirit?

5:19: Praise

Praise is the natural result of a devoted life to God. Joy will pour out from our heart. A Christian should be characterized by faith-filled optimism, happiness, and reverent worship. Their heart will be filled with psalms, hymns, and spiritual songs.

5:20: *Thankfulness*

This is a person who sees their blessings and will not hesitate to glorify God at every opportunity. This is a person who is full of love, joy, peace, gentleness, goodness, and faith.

5:21: *A Submissive Heart*

The *submitting* in this verse means "to arrange under." It is a military term expressing the idea of placing oneself under those responsible for you. The application is generic and applies universally. Christians are called to place themselves under each other. Our culture looks down on submission. The world sees it as a sign of weakness… something that should be avoided at all costs. Submission is not degrading. It is a fact of life. During New Testament times, the word was used to refer to the social ordering of people, such as warriors giving allegiance to their commander. Similarly, people living in a city, state, or region are to respect the authority of the local governor. Submission carries the responsibility to live in an orderly manner and not be seditious or rebellious.

From this, Paul elaborates in this text that "submission" should characterize the day-to-day life of the Christian. All believers "submit to one another." It is the outward expression of self-denial and concern for others. The absence of this virtue hinders the work of the Spirit inside us and in the local church.

The Heart of Submission

Philippians 2 contains some of the greatest teachings on submission and how it is expressed. In the opening verses, Paul lists out four expectations for the local church:

- 2:2a—think the same way.
- 2:2b—have the same love.
- 2:2c—(be) united in spirit.
- 2:2d—(be) intent on one purpose.

How is this possible? How can people get along so completely? The answer is found in the following two verses:

> Do nothing out of selfish ambition or conceit, but in humility consider others as more important than yourselves. Everyone should look not to his own interests, but rather to the interests of others, Philippians 2:3–4.

Here, we see the attitude that makes submission possible. It is characterized by humility, which is produced by the Spirit who dwells within us. As we are filled with the Spirit, Ephesians 5:18, we are being moved along the path to becoming more like God.

Submission in Day-to-Day Life

Some of the most practical instructions on submission come to us from Peter. In chapter 2, he reminds Christians of their place in this world (we are strangers and exiles, 2:11). Since that is the case, we are to conduct ourselves with honor through:

- 2:13—submitting to every human authority (emperors, governors, etc.)
- 2:15—doing good, living under the expectations of our Master.
- 2:17—honor everyone. Fear God. Honor the emperor.
- 2:18–20—submission also applies in the workplace.

In both examples, i.e., submission in public life and in the workplace, we may have to endure unjust treatment from cruel and godless people. The call here is to endure it. Not resist. Not rebel. But submit. *This brings favor with God*, 2:20. This certainly runs counter to the American way, which thrives on the promotion of one's personal rights and freedoms.

Next, Peter draws our attention to the greatest example of submission in the face of unjust treatment: Jesus. He *left (us) an example that (we) should follow in his steps,* 1 Peter 2:21. He did not respond to insults. He did not threaten. Instead, he trusted that God would right all the wrongs committed against him.

When one follows the example of Jesus, there will be submission in marriage, 1 Peter 3:1–6. The husband will respect and submit to his wife, 1 Peter 3:7. The principle of submission is undoubtedly seen in the directives of 1 Peter 3:8–12. How much would our relationships improve if we fulfilled these expectations more effectively?

Submission to Church Leaders

God has established shepherds as leaders in creating order in the local church. Their task is to *oversee* the work. They have been called to humbly lead the local church, exemplifying what it means to live the Christian life. Because of this, those who place them in this position are called to honor and respect their authority.

- Hebrews 13:17: *obey your leaders and submit to them, since they keep watch over your souls as those who will give an account, so they can do this with joy and not with grief, for that would be unprofitable for you.*
- 1 Peter 5:5: ... *be subject to the elders. All of you clothe yourselves with humility toward one another* ...
- 1 Corinthians 16:15b–16: here, we find a general principle of submission to leaders in the local church. Paul mentioned the household of Stephanas, who *had devoted themselves to serving the saints.* Paul then says, *I urge you to also submit to such people and to everyone who works and labors with them.*

It is the submissive attitude that makes the Christian life work.

For Thought and Reflection

1. What are the natural effects of being filled with the Spirit? (Ephesians 5:18–21)

2. What does it mean to submit? Why is it looked down upon in our culture?

3. What is the key ingredient to submission in our relationships? (See Philippians 2:3–4)

4. How can we better apply the principles of 1 Peter 2:13–17 as we think about the politics of our day? How can we better set an example of respect for our government leaders and people in the opposite party of our preference?

5. How does God expect us to treat our local church leaders? Why?

Lesson 10

Do Everything in the Name

And whatever you do, in word or in deed, do everything in the name of the Lord Jesus, giving thanks to God the Father through him, Colossians 3:17.

Introduction

Colossians 3:17 is the end of a line of thinking that began at 2:6–7, where Paul writes what some have called the thesis statement of Colossians:

So then, just as you have received Christ Jesus as Lord, continue to walk in him, being rooted and built up in him and established in the faith, just as you were taught, and overflowing with gratitude.

What is written here—a call for spiritual maturity—is the basis for which everything else in chapters 2–3 flows. When Paul says *walk in Him,* he is instructing our daily life and attitudes to reflect Christ. *Whoever says he abides in him ought to walk in the same way in which he walked,* 1 John 2:6.

We should also connect what is said at the beginning of Colossians 2:6. We have *received Christ Jesus as the Lord.* There is significance to the way Paul writes these words. It is seen more clearly in the original language. He says, "You have received Christ Jesus, *the* one who is *the* Lord." Christians embrace not just a message but a Person: Jesus Christ. He is the Lord of your life. He has the right to rule and the authority to determine and define what is honorable and righteous. His pleasure is to be the first thing we consider as we lead our life. No matter the situation,

His authority applies. So, we walk in union with Him, doing what He would do. How did Jesus walk?

- He walked in love.
- He walked in wisdom.
- He walked in truth.
- He walked in the Spirit.
- He walked in holiness.

Do these things describe the pattern of your life? In an increasing way?

Have we set our mind on things above, Colossians 3:1–2?

Have we put off the old person with all its old habits and sins, Colossians 3:5–9?

Are we committed to being renewed in the Spirit of our mind, Colossians 3:10?

Are we living consistently with our new reality of having been chosen, holy, and beloved, Colossians 3:12?

Whatever You Do

Now, let's connect Colossians 3:17. If we have received Christ Jesus as Lord, it would only make sense that we do everything in His name:

> And whatever you do, in word or in deed, do everything in the name of the Lord Jesus, giving thanks to God the Father through him.

The wording in the original language reads: "Whatever you do, whether in speech or action, do it all." Our English translations have filled in the expression to help us understand. Nothing escapes the kingship of Jesus because everything is now conducted in union with Him. Whatever we do, word, deed, everything, is to be done in His name.

This verse is a succinct summary of Christian living. It applies across the board to every thought, word, and deed. It has much more to do with our personal behavior and attitudes regarding our relationships with others in the local body than it does with authority in religious practices contrasted to denominationalism. We must keep the context in mind. This section focuses on our behavior in conjunction with other believers and people in the world. How do we treat them? How do we regard them? Everything we do needs to be consistent with the person of Jesus Christ.

No Codebook of Rules

The New Testament does not contain a codebook of rules. While sometimes we may wish we were left with more explicit details or regulations, the Spirit often left us with a set of principles, expecting us to ask ourselves, "What would Jesus do?" "Is this something I can engage in without compromising my influence for Christ?" "Can I do this thing *in the name of Christ*—whose reputation is at stake—in how I engage in my conduct?" "Will this thing bring glory to God, and can I do it out of a sense of gratitude and thankfulness for the opportunity of doing it?"

While there may be no specifics given, when we face these things with integrity, the person who allows Christ to rule their heart and actions will do the right thing. A listing of rules might sound convenient, but human history has proven man's ability to invent ways to get around rules and regulations. It is not as easy to get around the comprehensive statement of Christian duty that this verse provides.

If something confronts you and you are unsure if it would dishonor Christ, don't do it. If you are sure you can do it in submission to the Lord, in line with His Word, then do it joyfully and thankfully!

Speaking of Thankfulness

With everything we do, we need to be *giving thanks through Him to God the Father.* This applies even while we endure difficult circumstances, trusting that He is working through them to accomplish His intentions for us. We may not understand the "why" or know "how long," but we are committed to bringing Him glory in all situations. The opposite of thankfulness is grumbling. In the wilderness, the children of Israel grumbled continually—and it kept an entire generation from receiving the inheritance. Grumbling impugns the character of God. It implies either "God isn't good" or "He isn't in control of my life."

Thankfulness extends beyond Sunday to every day of our life. There is no division between the sacred and the secular for the Christian. Every day is another day to live thankfully under the dominion and authority of Jesus Christ. In every aspect of life, we can reflect the joy of salvation as we speak and act in the name of Christ.

Conclusion

Colossians 3:17 closes the line of thinking that began in 2:6. We represent Jesus in everything we do. He empowers us to do good. We cooperate with the direction the Spirit gives, with a spirit of gratefulness and thankfulness. God has done so much for us. Praise be to Him!

For Thought and Reflection

1. What does it mean to walk in Christ?

2. How does Colossians 3:17 connect back to the expectation of Colossians 2:6?

3. What is in the context of Colossians 3:17? How does the teaching of 3:12–14 apply in carrying out the directive of 3:17?

4. Why do you think the Spirit chose not to give us a codebook of rules … instead of giving us governing principles by which to live?

5. What is the opposite of thankfulness? Why is it condemned in Scripture? What are some things you can do to avoid it?

6. Did God design the Christian life to have a separation between the sacred and the secular? Explain?

7. What are some things you can do to more effectively carry out the expectation of Colossians 3:17?

Lesson 11

Look to the Interests of Others

Do nothing out of selfish ambition or conceit, but in humility consider others as more important than yourselves. Everyone should look not to his own interests, but rather to the interests of others, Philippians 2:3–4.

Introduction

O n the night before His death, Jesus identifies the fundamental characteristic of Christianity: *love.* He says that by it all will know that we are His disciples, John 13:34–35. This is the type of love that meets needs, often sacrificially. It is the opposite of the way the world loves, which usually loves in exchange for something it can receive. We are all familiar with the mentality: *I will love you as long as you give me something in return.* This type of love is often superficial and temporary. As circumstances and things change ... as life happens ... this type of love often evaporates like the morning dew.

In this lesson, we will examine one of the mountaintops of Paul's writing in the New Testament. The passage is written in the context of togetherness inside the local church family ... which is intended to be a sweet taste of what we will experience in heaven.

In Philippians 2:2, Paul wants his readers to draw on their common experiences in Christ and His grace. He stresses that we:

- Think the same way.
- Have the same love.
- Be united in spirit.
- Be intent on one purpose.

Christians need to be together with the same values and love. The heart characteristics described here come from the very core of our spiritual identity.

Philippians 2:3

This verse contains a negative and positive admonition. Let's look at the attitudes we are to resist:

Do nothing out of selfish ambition or conceit

Selfish ambition is translated as "selfishness" in the NASB and refers to self-seeking pursuits. It involves a strong ambition for personal success, no matter the cost. Today, we might describe it as an attitude of *I'm gonna get what I want no matter what it takes.* Selfishness is often the cause of envy and rivalry. It is a self-seeking spirit that leads to quarreling, hassling, haggling, fighting, arguing, and contending.

The selfish person is, more often than not, at war with everyone else because they are being dominated by the flesh. Their relationships are characterized by jealousy, strife, and conflict. Selfish people are driven to promote their cause, interests, or pet projects when they allow the flesh to take over. We must, at all costs, eliminate selfish ambition from our lives.

Conceit is a state of mind that seeks personal glory. A conceited person will do what they must in order to make their opinion known. We might describe a conceited person as one who engages in arrogant self-promotion. The conceited person continually provokes and puts down others to gain the highest place. Conceit and pride go hand in hand. Someone has described pride as *camel-nosed,* i.e., "high-blown, puffed-up, stiff-necked, aloof, lofty, inaccessible, seeking to tower over others."[40]

---

40   Cooper, Dale. "The Wardrobe of Easter: Humility." Online. Retrieved 01/02/23 from https://worship.calvin.edu/resources/resource-library/the-wardrobe-of-easter-humility

Other words that go with it are "inordinate self-esteem, egotism, self-glorification, vainglory, and vanity."

The exhortation in v. 3 is to remove these things. Conceit and pride rank among the deadliest, most debilitating of the seven cardinal sins of Proverbs 6:16–19.

Be Humble

In humility consider others as more important than yourselves. This is the corrective for the two previous negatives. "Humility" has an interesting history behind it. During Paul's time, the word was used to describe the mentality of a slave, i.e., it was a term of derision. The pagan world saw a humble person as someone who was unfit, low, common, or useless. Humility was seen as an ugly quality, something never to be sought after or admired. Lowliness and weakness were seen as shameful. Great men were those who overcame those traits through noble acts and thoughts.

And yet, it is the first virtue Jesus teaches in the sermon on the mount: *Blessed are the poor in spirit, for the kingdom of heaven is theirs,* Matthew 5:3. For the worldly-minded person who is all about looking impressive in the eyes of others, this is like hearing nails on a chalkboard. It is the exact opposite of human nature. Notice how Paul defines the word in our text. Humility is when we make the decision to count others as more important than ourselves. It is the very opposite of selfish ambition and conceit. It is a realistic appraisal of oneself and others as being in the image of God. It is an attitude that is expressed by positive action. We allow the needs of others to surpass our own. We do this by:

- Respecting them
- Listening to them
- Serving them
- Speaking good about them

- Strengthening them
- Encouraging them[41]

Philippians 2:4

Everyone should look not to his own interests but rather to the interests of others. This verse spells out how the previous verse works. The primary aim or goal of our life is to become involved in the lives of others and their cause. Again, this is in total contrast with the world that emphasizes the worship and promotion of self. Instead, we are to "look," which means to pay careful attention. Paul does not mean here that we should completely neglect ourselves, but we need to reprioritize our lives so that the greater share is focused on others. Their needs and concerns must surpass our own.

"Interests" in 2:4 is a filler word. Young's Literal Translation says, "each not to your own look."[42] It's an open-ended statement. Today, we would say, "Let each look not to your own "_____ _____." (Fill in the blank.) That blank could be your finances, property, family, reputation, success, or happiness. We are to be concerned about the things of others.

We could rightly connect v. 4 back to Matthew 22:39, where Jesus recites the second greatest commandment: *you shall love your neighbor as yourself.*

How can you make the good of others the focus of your life?

---

41   Hansen, G. Walter. *The Letter to the Philippians.* The Pillar New Testament Commentary. Grand Rapids, MI; Nottingham, England: William B. Eerdmans Publishing Company, 2009, p. 115.

42   Young, Robert. *Young's Literal Translation.* Bellingham, WA: Logos Bible Software, 1997.

- Who is a widow or widower you can spend time with?
- Who is a young person you can take under your wing?
- What young newlywed couple could use some guidance and encouragement?
- Who can you go to and pray with?
- Who is going through a valley that you can join with and walk through it together with them?

When you do this, you are literally changing your life *and* the life of someone else. It is not about where they are presently in life; it is about whether you will count others as worthy of your help and encouragement. Will you serve your brothers and sisters? Will you make the time to do what builds them up?

The Perfect Example

To learn humility, all we must do is look to Jesus. *Let this mind be in you which was in Christ Jesus,* Paul says in v. 5. Our Savior and brother, Jesus, loved us, forgave us, died for us, accepted us, justified us, and made us heirs of an eternal kingdom … when He owed us nothing. He counted us worthy when we weren't worthy. He counted us greater than Himself.

> For who is greater, the one at the table or the one serving? Isn't it the one at the table? But I am among you as the one who serves, Luke 22:27.

For Thought and Reflection

1. What is the fundamental characteristic of Christianity? How does it fit in with the content of this lesson?

2. What is the primary context of Philippians 1:27–2:4?

3. How would you define *selfish ambition* and *conceit?* While there may be some overlap, what is the difference between the two?

4. How was the virtue of humility viewed by the Greco-Roman world?

5. Is humility an attitude or action or both? Explain.

6. How can you express your humility?

7. What does it mean to esteem the interests of others more than your own?

8. In what way did Jesus set the perfect example of humility?

Lesson 12

Make Things Right
with Your Brother

So if you are offering your gift on the altar, and there you remember that your brother or sister has something against you, leave your gift there in front of the altar. First go and be reconciled with your brother or sister, and then come and offer your gift. Reach a settlement quickly with your adversary while you're on the way with him to the court, or your adversary will hand you over to the judge, and the judge to the officer, and you will be thrown into prison. Truly I tell you, you will never get out of there until you have paid the last penny, Matthew 5:23–26.

Introduction

If you want to see a person in their best character, it is seen when they forgive. *A person's discretion makes him slow to anger, and it is his glory to overlook an offense,* Proverbs 19:11. When we choose to forgive, we reflect the character of God, who *forgives iniquity* and *delights in unfailing love,* Micah 7:18. It is in the heart of God to forgive, and it is this type of heart He calls on us to develop. Paul says it this way in Colossians 3:13:

> bearing with one another and forgiving one another if anyone has a grievance against another. Just as the Lord has forgiven you, so you are also to forgive.

How eager should we be to forgive others if we have been forgiven of everything? We must learn how to do it because people are going to need it. We are all human and prone to weakness and mistakes.

Today's lesson is based on the text in Jesus' Sermon on the Mount. Leading up to our main text, Jesus has discussed how He came to fulfill the law—not destroy it. In the rest of Matthew 5, Jesus will illustrate a very important principle underlying our behavior and attitudes: *the spirit of the law matters more than the letter.* One of the first examples He uses is on the matter of holding on to anger.

In Matthew 5:21, Jesus quotes the 6th commandment, Exodus 20:13. He also quotes their addition to the law by saying whoever killed would be in danger of judgment. The "judgment" in view here is the one by the local courts of the day. Jesus is pointing out how they had reduced the law to nothing more than a legal violation. *Commit murder? There will be certain punitive consequences that follow.* In so doing, they changed the law to a negative, which caused them to feel good about themselves because they had not committed murder.

We, too, must guard against doing the same. If we are not careful, we can define the law negatively. We see this problem throughout the New Testament. There was a time in Paul's life when he felt he was keeping the law perfectly because he defined his righteousness by what he didn't do. The rich young ruler of Matthew 19 and the Pharisee of Luke 18:11 also fit into this category.

What does Jesus intend to teach us in this part of the Sermon on the Mount?

The Spirit of the Law is What Matters

Now let's look at verse 22.

> But I tell you, everyone who is angry with his brother or sister will be subject to judgment. Whoever insults his brother or sister, will be subject to the court. Whoever says, 'You fool!' will be subject to hellfire.

What Jesus wants us to understand is that one must not only kill, but he must not be angry without a cause. Anger is a God-given emotion that is justified in circumstances of disapproval over evil, matters of self-defense, or being upset over sinful behavior. Scripture records instances of both God and Jesus being angry[43], so the emotion is not sinful in and of itself. But this is not the type of anger Jesus has in mind here. He is speaking of bitter hatred and resentment which often leads to harsh talk and acts of unkindness.

We must guard against speaking words of contempt. The older translations use the word *raca* here, which is a strong insult against another person. There is no exact modern equivalent to this word. Those who used this word were calling the other person "worthless," "shallow-brained," "senseless," "blockhead," or "silly fool," etc. Jesus is teaching that to slander another person is equal to slandering God Himself and equivalent to murdering that person. *Contempt is murder of the heart.*[44] Jesus goes on to call out a person who vilifies another person. This often arises from a bitter, hateful, and/or resentful heart. The word *fool* (moros) comes from the word we use today for *moron*. It often had to do with a person who was both godless and stubborn.

Did you see the progression in v. 22? Anger is the underlying motive behind murder. Slander is even more serious because it expresses that anger in a hurtful and malicious way. Finally, to condemn a person's character by calling them a fool is even more serious. Again, the problem Jesus is trying to correct here is the expression of hatred and malicious things out of unbridled anger. Doing so is the equivalent of murder and places us in danger of hell.

---

43   See Psalm 7:11; Mark 3:5.

44   MacArthur, *Matthew*, p. 294.

Holding on to These Sinful Things Negatively Impacts Our Worship

So if you are offering your gift on the altar, and there you remember that your brother or sister has something against you, leave your gift there in front of the altar. First go and be reconciled with your brother or sister, and then come and offer your gift, Matthew 5:23–24.

Sins of anger and hatred do have an impact on our relationship with God. Not only are we not to be angry without cause, but we are also expected to move in a positive manner to make things right with someone we have wronged. Reconciliation comes before worship. We must not stop at "I must not murder" or "I must not insult someone." We need to train our hearts not to think evil by taking the proper steps to remove the trouble.

Sometimes, we may attempt to atone for our moral failings by trying to tip the scales back in our favor with some good deed or action. *I've done this wrong; I'll just go worship God—that'll take care of it.* Jesus says, go to the one you have wronged before you go to worship. We must get things in the open before God and before the person(s) we have hurt. Unresolved conflict between you and a brother or sister must be settled before engaging in worship. To neglect to do this makes one hypocritical by asking for forgiveness without repentance. We need to be willing to do everything we can to make things right, regardless of who is responsible for the problem in the relationship. What the other person does or how they respond does not matter. Our first responsibility is our own compliance to the will of God. Holding on to a grudge, coddling resentfulness, or building hatred impacts your worship with God:

If I had been aware of malice in my heart, the Lord would not have listened, Psalm 66:18.

Samuel asked Saul …

> Does the Lord take pleasure in burnt offerings and sacrifices
> as much as in obeying the Lord? Look: to obey is better than
> sacrifice, to pay attention is better than the fat of rams, 1 Samuel
> 15:22.

Matters of Reconciliation Are Urgent

> Reach a settlement quickly with your adversary while you're
> on the way with him to the court, or your adversary will hand
> you over to the judge, and the judge to the officer, and you will
> be thrown into prison. Truly I tell you, you will never get out of
> there until you have paid the last penny, Matthew 5:25–26.

These verses are further illustrations of the principle just spelled out previously. Make things right as soon as possible. Time is always moving forward. Days turn into weeks and weeks into years. Life is fragile. You never know when your life will end … or the life of the other person will end. As we go through the journey of life, God requires us to think about the relationships we have with others. Is there bad blood? Are things not as they should be? The emphasis is to settle them at once. Tomorrow is not guaranteed, and Jesus emphasizes that you do not want to enter the judgment like that. The time for reconciliation is always *now*.

Conclusion

Disciples of Jesus are to have the highest regard for their fellow man … especially those closest to them, i.e., family and brethren. We are to respect the sanctity of human life and address the differences we have with others through the practice of love. *Love covers a multitude of sins,* 1 Peter 4:8. There is never any justification for us to put down another person. While we may have never murdered anyone, we must kill our inner attitudes that hold on to anger and hate and express themselves through destructive words and hostility. We need to figure out ways to resolve our anger by other means than focusing on personalities we don't mesh with through destructive attitudes toward them. Remember Ephesians 4:26: *be angry … and sin not.*

So:

- Take the initiative in reconciliation.
- Be willing to forgive, as you have been forgiven.
- Pray for the one who has wronged you.
- Focus on something besides the problem that derailed your relationship.
- Practice brotherly love … and keep no record of wrongs suffered.

For Thought and Reflection

1. Why do you think developing a heart of forgiveness is so difficult for us?

2. What does God teach us about forgiveness?

3. What does it mean that the spirit of the law matters more than the letter?

4. How can we be guilty today of turning the law into mostly negatives? What kind of attitude does this lead to?

5. What is the point of Jesus' teaching in 5:22–23?

6. Why is holding on to bitterness and resentment such a serious matter? (5:23–24)

7. Why must this problem be dealt with urgency?

8. What are some things you can do to become a more forgiving person?

Lesson 13

Work Heartily—As to the Lord

Slaves, obey your human masters in everything. Don't work only while being watched, as people-pleasers, but work wholeheartedly, fearing the Lord. Whatever you do, do it from the heart, as something done for the Lord and not for people, knowing that you will receive the reward of an inheritance from the Lord. You serve the Lord Christ. For the wrongdoer will be paid back for whatever wrong he has done, and there is no favoritism. Masters, deal with your slaves justly and fairly, since you know that you too have a Master in heaven, Colossians 3:22–4:1.

Introduction

Beginning with Colossians 3:22 and continuing through 4:6, Paul addresses Christian relationships with those outside the family. In all these experiences, the driving force is Christ. As mentioned in Colossians 3:17, Christians *do everything in the name of the Lord Jesus.* No matter what status we find ourselves in life, our Lord is at the forefront. In serving one's master, the slave would be expected to ask, "What would Jesus do here?" "Is my service to my master something I engage in without compromising my influence for Christ?" "Will my behavior bring glory to God, and can I live all my life with a sense of gratitude and thankfulness for the opportunity of doing it?" These are the guiding principles that are to govern our life... Jesus is to shape any and every relationship we find ourselves in. We have given our lives in submission to Him. He has the supreme authority over our life.

The beauty of this passage (and its companion in Ephesians 6:5–9) is that God is completely impartial. God does not care about the social position of the master or the slave. The cross has made every person equal and challenges them to live a new life looking forward to *an inheritance from the Lord,* 3:24. A few paragraphs before, Paul writes:

> In Christ there is not Greek and Jew, circumcision and uncircumcision, barbarian, Scythian, slave and free; but Christ is all and in all, Colossians 3:11.

This is the beauty of Christianity. The most important thing is to live a godly life that brings glory to Christ no matter the circumstance. Today, the application of these verses fits well inside the relationship between an employer and his employees. How should we conduct ourselves in this relationship?

A tragedy of our time is how the basic principles of respect and recognizing the authority of others over us is ignored. At all levels of employment … from the one who performs menial tasks to the executive level … many engage much of their time in gossip and malicious talk about those who are over them and only work when the boss is near. Many productive hours are lost to wasted time on the Internet, standing around, or idle talk. Required tasks deemed unimportant can be ignored. Scheduled work hours are called off for dishonest reasons. When I worked for a large retailer during my undergrad years, some of my co-workers would hide in the stockroom to avoid doing work. My understanding is that things are much worse today than three decades ago. More and more, I hear employers talk about how it is hard to find reliable, trustworthy workers who demonstrate integrity and character.

Shame on us. We must do better with subsequent generations to ensure these principles are ingrained in our young people. We have much work to do.

Do Your Work from the Heart—Fearing the Lord

Notice as you read verse 22 how Paul calls for genuine service and obedience to those who have authority over us. We obey them *in everything,* whether the responsibility is something we enjoy or not. When assigned a task, we are to give ourselves *wholeheartedly* to it, 3:22c. It does not matter if we think it is unnecessary, ridiculous, or silly. We agreed when we went to work to fulfill the responsibilities of the job.

The Christian is someone who gives himself or herself totally to the task—*all the time*—not just doing the minimum to avoid a write-up or other disciplinary actions, 3:22b. Our work is not just about what we want our employer to see. Our work is about what the Lord sees … which includes our motives and thoughts. If we are mere people-pleasers, not only are we disrespecting our boss, but more importantly, we are demonstrating no reverence for the Lord who has called us to an authentic display of Christian virtues. We are to serve our employer *from the heart,* 3:23a. We are to work this way no matter if our boss is two-faced, dishonest, regards us as nothing, or flat-out evil. Why is this so?

We Work for the Lord, Not for People

Lenski adequately captures the essence of Paul's writing in his comments when he says, *throw your soul into the word as if your one employer were the Lord!*[45] Why is this so important to keep in mind? First, we work, *fearing the Lord,* 3:22d. It's not just about our self-preservation or interests; we work with the understanding that we will answer to Him on the last day for all we have done or said.

> For we must all appear before the judgment seat of Christ,
> so that each may be repaid for what he has done in the body,
> whether good or evil. Therefore, since we know the fear of the

45   Lenski, R. C. H. *The Interpretation of St. Paul's Epistles to the Colossians, to the Thessalonians, to Timothy, to Titus and to Philemon.* Columbus, OH: Lutheran Book Concern, 1937, p. 184.

Lord, we try to persuade people. What we are is plain to God, and I hope it is also plain to your consciences, 2 Corinthians 5:11–12.

The apostles taught that God expects obedience in all things … whether good or not so good. Why this is necessary brings up the second point we need to remember.

How we work lets other people know how serious we are about the practice of Christianity.

At work, do I adorn Christ in everything?

> Slaves are to submit to their masters in everything, and to be well-pleasing, not talking back or stealing, but demonstrating utter faithfulness, so that they may adorn the teaching of God our Savior in everything, Titus 2:0–10

At work, do I honor my boss as worthy of respect? If I do not, do I realize how my attitude reflects on Jesus Christ?

> All who are under the yoke as slaves should regard their own masters as worthy of all respect so that God's name and his teaching will not be blasphemed. Let those who have believing masters not be disrespectful to them because they are brothers, but serve them even better, since those who benefit from their service are believers and dearly loved. Teach and encourage these things, 1 Timothy 6:1–2.

At work, am I following in the steps of Christ … even if I am being treated unfairly?

> Household slaves, submit to your masters with all reverence not only to the good and gentle ones but also to the cruel. For it brings favor if, because of a consciousness of God, someone endures grief from suffering unjustly. For what credit is there if

when you do wrong and are beaten, you endure it? But when you do what is good and suffer, if you endure it, this brings favor with God. For you were called to this, because Christ also suffered for you, leaving you an example, that you should follow in his steps, 1 Peter 2:18–21.

God calls us to be obedient to Him in all things.

We Work Toward an Inheritance from the Lord

Sometimes, it is easy to become cynical. Our minds tell us that if we left our job tomorrow, there would be someone to fill our shoes the next day, and the company would go on like we were never there. And on its most basic level, that is true. But this is never an excuse to back off on our responsibility. The Christian works for others knowing that even if he or she does not receive a reward for their service, they trust that God will repay them for their faithfulness, 3:24a. *The dead will be judged according to their works by what is written in the books,* Revelation 20:12–13. Whatever a believer does for the Savior here on earth will never be regretted. So, as employees, we must always remember that it is the Lord Jesus Christ we serve, 3:24b. We can trust in His reward. See Luke 19:11–27; James 1:12; and 2 Timothy 4:7–8. The question is, will we keep our mind elevated on the spiritual—even as we must trudge through in patience with the day-to-day grind of work? *Set* your mind on the Lord, Colossians 3:2!

If we do wrong, there will be consequences, 3:25. We will reap what we sow, Galatians 6:7. Ultimately when final judgment comes, there will be no favoritism with God. If we treat others wrongly, we should fear. If we have been treated wrongly, we should trust that God will make all things right.

A Word to Employers

The bulk of Paul's instructions in Colossians have to do with the slave (employee in today's application).

> Masters, deal with your slaves justly and fairly, since you know that you too have a Master in heaven, Colossians 4:1.

First, let's think about the historical perspective of the first century and how revolutionary Paul's words would be. Slaves were also human beings with fundamental rights. This would have been extraordinary and really have caught the attention of his audience.

Now, let's make the application to today. Employers, how should you treat your employees? Paul says to treat them *justly* and *fairly.* The implication in the second part of the verse is that God will judge those who mistreat those under them. When dealing with an employee, one must ask, how would Jesus desire that I treat them? Employers are themselves slaves of the one Master, Jesus Christ.

Conclusion

In whatever role a Christian finds himself or herself ... at home or at work ... life must be lived *for the Lord* and in harmony with those around. Taking the principle of Ephesians 5:21 into consideration, we *submit to everyone out of reverence for Christ.* How effective are you in recognizing His authority *and* the authority of others who have been placed over you?

For Thought and Reflection

1. How do the principles of Colossians 3:17 fit into what Paul expresses in Colossians 3:22–4:1?

2. On what basis are all Christians equal? Does God have regard for social/economic status? Explain. How does this understanding help us to look at one another in Christ, and all humans for that matter?

3. In what things are we to obey those who have authority over us? Is how we feel about what is expected of us something that matters?

4. What type of consistency is expected out of the way we work? What type of attitude does God want? Explain.

5. To whom do we work for?

6. Why do we serve Him *out of fear?*

7. What can we expect for faithful service?

8. In what way should an employer treat his employees?

www.ingramcontent.com/pod-product-compliance
Lightning Source LLC
Chambersburg PA
CBHW042337040426

42447CB00017B/3460